BR *in the*
EIGHTIES

BR *in the* EIGHTIES

David St John Thomas
& Patrick Whitehouse

with contributions also based on the work of

Michael Bonavia
Colin Boocock
Murray Brown
John Gough
Chris Heaps
Howard Johnston
Geoffrey Kichenside
Brian Perren
Paul Shannon
David Wilcock
Neil Wooler

DAVID & CHARLES
Newton Abbot London

ACKNOWLEDGEMENTS

The authors would like to thank John Edgington, John Powell and John Smart for the trouble they have taken to read through the manuscript and assist with the selection as well as the captioning of the photographs. In this respect it has been possible to call on expertise from the National Railway Museum, one time serving railway officer and a knowledgeable modern historian. With a complex book taking in a full decade of change this help has been vital and appreciated.

THE 1980s AND 1990s

This book is specifically on the 1980s and does not intend to continue the story into the beginning of the 1990s, although in passing it may be noted that Sectorisation led to a June 1990 decision to abolish the Regions and that at the time we go to press British Rail are entering another period of less buoyant business with sharp traffic decline notably in parts of Network SouthEast.

(Page 2) Lancashire & Yorkshire legacy. Class 504 Nos 77168 and 65447 pass Queen's Road signalbox, Manchester, forming the 14.00 Bury–Manchester Victoria service on 3 May 1989 over this 1,200v dc route. The two-car unit is in Greater Manchester orange and brown livery.

Merseyrail Northern Line. A busy scene at Kirkdale in November 1988 with No 508136 working an Ormskirk service while No 507004 arrives on a Kirkby to Liverpool train.

British Library Cataloguing in Publication Data

Thomas, David St John
BR in the eighties.
1. Great Britain. Railway services: British Rail
I. Title   II. Whitehouse, Patrick, 1922
385.0941

ISBN 0-7153-9854-7

Typeset by Typesetters (Birmingham) Ltd
and printed in Singapore
by C. S. Graphics Pte Ltd
for David & Charles plc
Brunel House   Newton Abbot   Devon

CONTENTS

25kV emu No 310103, carrying the Midline logo, passes the site of Monument Lane depot as it enters Birmingham with a local service for Coventry in May 1989. Building work on this site has now extended the tunnel to St Vincent's Rd bridge where the picture was taken.

Class 303 emu No 303046, in Strathclyde livery, leaves Glasgow Central with the 17.27 to Gourock on 11 June 1988.

Unique Electric. Brush-built Co-Co Class 89 No 89001 (now named Avocet) stands in platform No 1 at King's Cross in 1988.

The mainstay of the ECML InterCity service through the decade has been the HST sets, providing fast and popular trains under the IC 125 banner, foundations upon which electrification with IC 225 can build. The 11.00 King's Cross–Aberdeen HST (No 43094 trailing) sweeps round the curve at Penmanshiel on 13 September 1987.

1
THE AGE OF THE TRAIN

THREE-quarters of the track including half the through lines, the semaphore signals, the last vestiges of freight facilities and the last of the men who used proudly to work for the old railway company have gone, yet the long-distance service is faster, more frequent and above all better used than at any time in railway history, and the number of passengers passing through probably at an all time high. The comment happens to be about the writer's home station, but much of it might equally apply to numerous others.

One thing is for certain. The eighties was not the decade in which people abandoned railways, not anyway in Britain. Virtually everywhere from the Highlands to London's suburbs, main line and local, passenger trains were steadily busier, the total number carried exceeding that of pre-Beeching days when the system was much larger. Indeed, the vast majority of lines remaining carried record numbers of passengers for peacetime on ordinary working days, the great holiday and excursion tidal waves of traffic of course being history. The statement is truer of lines than individual stations since average journey lengths are much longer, and continued to increase during the eighties. And while BR gave up carrying more categories of goods and our daily newspapers overnight, the overall freight picture again improved to a greater extent than most people forecast. If newspaper trains ceased to cause nocturnal activity over much of the system, the number of travelling Post Offices actually increased.

The eighties was a decade of paradoxes, great and small. As the government squeezed the finances ever harder, British Rail became more efficient, and while even InterCity began by pruning 10 per cent of its mileage, at the end most of the sectors were more concerned about how to handle their increasing traffic. As financial results improved and there was increasing reason to believe the slogan on everyone's lips at the decade's start, 'This is the age of the train', morale deteriorated further. While much was achieved in improving safety standards, towards the decade's end there was a series of accidents that perhaps shocked the public more than anything since Harrow & Wealdstone in the very early days of nationalisation. And while the eighties saw fewer closures and many more reopenings than anyone could reasonably have hoped, it ended with thunder clouds of uncertainty about management style, privatisation, how to solve overcrowding, the Channel Tunnel.

Then there was the paradox that the erstwhile Premier Line out of Euston steadily slipped down the speed and performance league as the High Speed Trains out of King's Cross, St Pancras and Paddington proved (for all the

Class 50 No 50021 Rodney leaves Newton Abbot with the 10.30 Liverpool to Penzance train on 10 March 1987 a few weeks before the removal of the semaphore signals.

The 1980s certainly proved to be the age of the train, but not the age of the APT as this entrance barrier at Glasgow Central proclaims in May 1983.

Manchester Pullman. No 86244 The Royal British Legion (named 2 November 1981) gets away from Crewe with the 16.00 ex-Euston on 16 August 1988. The rake is mostly Mk3A and Mk3B (1985 Pullman) coaches. The last BR all-Pullman service, to Manchester, ceased in May 1985.

Class 31 No 31468 and Class 47 No 47010 receive attention in the maintenance area of Crewe diesel depot on 22 June 1988.

A pair of Class 20s, Nos 20007 and 20053, struggle up the steep incline out of Coalbrookdale with an empty MGR train on 3 November 1988. This freight line has seen a limited summer weekend passenger service to a temporary station at Coalbrookdale for the Ironbridge museums since 1987.

No 37669 in early Railfreight grey livery brings a down English China Clays train, consisting of newly introduced CDA wagons, into Lostwithiel station on 6 May 1988.

No 87028 Lord President *displays its InterCity livery while pausing at Carlisle with a southbound express on 27 August 1988. It does not carry the swallow symbol.*

undoubted technical troubles) that they could sustain their role as InterCity's workaday tool. Catering that had been so under threat in the later seventies suddenly attracted new importance; indeed, the single Manchester Pullman that looked almost certain to be a casualty of further standardisation in the eighties was joined by a bevy of Pullmans if only Pullman service on HSTs and Mark 3s. But it became clear that the passenger was not automatically right: only when he paid up! Thus while first-class patronage was encouraged, and more businessmen complained bitterly that they had to go first-class in order to enjoy their British breakfast, more humble individuals who merely wanted to enjoy the view from the train were not so generously treated. It was perhaps the miracle of the decade that BR was allowed to invest so heavily in a new generation of multiple units. Enthusiasts were less surprised that much of that investment went sour through design faults and technical failures, and grieved that so little thought was given to the simple, old fashioned matter of looking out, the deprivation of forward and backward view that had encouraged so much travel on the first generation of multiple units allegedly being due to the unions not liking the public seeing their men at work. Not that the working man's point of view has been generally well heard.

12

Management-union relations were of course at the heart of many developments. Once private enterprise was excluded in passionate principle. If Travellers Fare did not wish to provide a service on a train, there should be none; if they closed a refreshment room, it had to lie idle for a year before a private operator was allowed to take over. The eighties brought commercial pragmatism, with for example many refreshment-trolley services run by private firms that employees of any organisation as large as BR would almost certainly have found impractical. In all kinds of ways many bad old practices disappeared, while at last the central administrative overhead came under control. Generally, and one says it graciously, sectorisation has worked, the eighties seeing it flowering and bringing both improvements and cost savings. InterCity has its own clear identity, though the greatest achievements have perhaps been with Network SouthEast, where the tide has really turned, and in Provincial with its own increasing network of imaginative expresses often resulting from stringing several services together. Suddenly many stations have through services to many more destinations.

The need to emphasise that God would not maintain the system indefinitely

Two veteran campaigners. Class 40 No 40160 tows a failed Class 108 dmu near Seascale on a Barrow-Carlisle service. Both designs first appeared in 1958 and by the 1980s were showing signs of their age. The photograph is dated 15 June 1984; No 40160 was withdrawn in November.

Jubilee Class 4-6-0 No 5593
Kolhapur *rounds the curve into
Rotherham Masborough station
(now closed) en route from
Birmingham to Carnforth via York
and Leeds on 4 June 1988.*

*The crisp Highland air makes for a
fine display of steam from K1 No
2005 as it hauls the Royal
Scotsman along the shore of Loch
Eil on the Fort William to Mallaig
line in 1988.*

The skyline of Bridgnorth, dominated by Telford's church tower, provides the backdrop for this view of Class 59 No 59001 Yeoman Endeavour *leaving the Severn Valley terminus with a train for Kidderminster on the SVR diesel weekend in May 1988.*

Parcels sector locomotive No 47567 Red Star *leaves Carlisle with the Hadrian Special on the return journey to King's Cross via the Settle & Carlisle line in June 1988.*

THE AGE OF THE TRAIN

no matter what restrictive practices and losses could hardly have been greater. Yet this writer's abiding impression of the eighties is that management along with the government did not know when to stop. Yes, there has been more consistency, a following of the capitalist competitive dream, which has paid good dividends. But the pressure for productivity has sometimes been remorseless. Generally the culture has lacked colour and personality, certainly fun and pride on the job. Improving ratios might have satisfied officials at headquarters but have only produced harder work and often more complaints from the public for the railwayman out on the system. To a large extent this is perhaps inevitably a criticism of the chairman from September 1983, Robert Reid. But then another paradox is that he was successful in persuading the government to allow increased investment, especially in rolling stock.

Sir Peter Parker who he replaced will always be remembered as an enthusiastic chairman with a human touch. The 'This is the age of the train' slogan thoroughly suited him. He will not however go down in financial history as a great achiever, and it has to be said (as recorded later in these pages) that even under his leadership labour relations were far from perfect. That Sir Robert Reid has been more effective is one of the headlines of the eighties. He proved himself to be thoroughly professional as a railwayman and ruthless as a manager. But the pips squeaked and still the remorseless pressure was on . . . and on, in a cool, impersonal style. Any joyous note there was came very occasionally from the sector managers, but they were seen as too much under corporate control to exercise real individuality of style.

The Clapham accident of December 1988, the first for half a century in Britain due to the failure of the signalling, appalled the public in demonstrating how poor morale and discipline were in a vital part of the service at a key point. The industrial labour dispute of early summer 1989 had virtually the whole public ridiculing BR's labour relations and calling for a change of style. It was a sad but inevitable outcome of not maintaining a proper balance between productivity and personality. Those who used large parts of the system regularly saw from daily observation that many staff enjoyed ever less satisfaction. Everyone has his own story of being ignored when requesting information and of being left uncertain what to do when things have gone wrong, such as connections lost. Management decidedly cannot rely on having its spokesmen on the spot in the shape of co-operative station staff.

Which is not to say that much fine work is not achieved. Driving standards on the whole improved during the eighties and certainly average speeds increased, in some cases dramatically. The overnight maintenance work on HSTs in particular deserves the award of many medals. Though frequently finding some initial reason to put you, the customer, down, restaurant-car stewards then generally look after you well, and enjoying good food at speed remains one of the joys of railway travel. It is just that it could have been more meaningful and less unpleasant had it felt a touch more like a pilgrimage than a harsh, faceless drive for productivity. Even the lack of a catchy slogan

at the decade's end ('The age of the train's' replacement 'We're getting there' only lasted briefly) contributes to this lack of social purpose.

What will the enthusiast's main memories be of the eighties? Not, to be sure, the rapid changes in administrative structure, much though the results of sectorisation have been felt actually on the track. One memory will certainly be of the running of far more steam trains than seemed possible in the seventies, not all of them successful . . . the GWR 150 specials, the Blackmore Vales, Cambrian Coasts, Cumbrian Mountains and regulars for some seasons into Scarborough and over the West Highland. While ordinary motive power generally became more standardised, and again as told later in these pages the difference between locomotive-hauled and multiple-unit stock less marked, the variety still remains impressive and just as many notebooks and cameras record the passage of trains at the end as at the beginning of the eighties. Liveries have of course proliferated; not since pre-1923 days have so many different colour schemes been seen, the only snag being that often

Class 37 hauled freight. Nos 37077 British Steel Shelton *and 37096 double head the 10.50 Lackenby to Corby 'steel-liner' train through Cargo Fleet, Middlesbrough on 9 December 1986.*

With the advent of 110 mph running on the West Coast main line a number of Mk1 gangwayed full brakes (fitted with B4 bogies) coded NHA were specially maintained for high-speed running. No 92032 is seen here at Crewe in September 1989.

Alexander/Barclay Class 143 dmu No 143022 in Tyne and Wear PTE colours crosses the High Level bridge into Gateshead with the 14.17 Newcastle to Middlesbrough service on 7 November 1986.

The original narrow-bodied Leyland/BREL Class 141 dmu consisting of Nos 55503/55523 approaches Heaton Lodge Junction, Mirfield with the 14.51 Leeds to Marsden train on 21 March 1987. The set sports West Yorkshire PTE colours.

No 47475 rounds the curve at King Edward Bridge Junction, Gateshead with the 10.23 Newcastle–Liverpool Lime Street on 16 May 1989. Both locomotive and train are in Provincial colours. The leading vehicles are a Mk1 gangwayed full brake carried on B4 bogies and a Mk2A corridor first. Note the Metro bridge in the background.

Class 58 locomotives Nos 58016, 58017 and 58018 under construction inside Doncaster works on 28 July 1984. They were taken into BR stock in October 1984 and allocated to Toton depot.

two or more liveries are included in the same train where for example the PTE's dedicated stock gets diverted.

Most of the semaphores of 1980 have gone, virtually no large gantries remaining in total use. But multiple-aspect signalling has not been (nor ever will be) universal. Radio signalling made more than a debut, helping toward the achievement of one of the decade's miracles, not only the survival but with greater expectation of long life of much of the Highland lines and many more. Indeed, no major routes closed in the eighties. Survivals include the Cambrian Coast, radio signalled in 1988, where Barmouth viaduct was after all repaired, the Central Wales where a decision was taken to rebuild the bridge which collapsed while a train was crossing it in high flood, and the Settle & Carlisle where the government perhaps surprisingly refused closure.

Another memory must surely be of the improvement to many stations, some of the London termini becoming shopping meccas, albeit the reduction in size of key ones such as Crewe and the general simplification of track layouts. The wartime hunt for German spies was not carried out with greater enthusiasm than the campaign to eliminate diamond crossings! Station improvements, and most of the reopenings, of course resulted from that new pragmatic combination of railway, municipal and industrial sponsorship. Repainting schemes in particular have been more imaginative, and for example one can proudly take overseas visitors interested in railways around our great cathedrals of the steam age now doing record business in a whole variety of ways . . . more trains and passengers, more refreshment facilities, many more shopping complexes.

What you cannot turn to with such pride is BR's printed timetable, which changed format several times during the eighties and ended as a poor thing, well below continental standards. Throughout the eighties some officials displayed a tendency to overdo the latest idea, often itself not particularly sound. Thus we were told that, since the timetable was only used 'by enthusiasts and the travel trade', it was pointless to indicate which trains had meal service, and while vital to show which services were operated by Sprinters nobody was interested in which were HSTs. Then long-term account holders were told that when they reached sixty they could no longer use BR's own rail warrants but had to switch to credit cards on which a commission is payable. BR's own credit card experiment at the decade's start failed through sheer ineptitude. It is not hard to portray the BR of the eighties Monty Python style with such stupidities as creating a semi-autonomous Cornish Railways with great enthusiasm one year only to abandon them the next as though that were equally great progress. Happily achievements do take place alongside such nonsense.

Railfreight-liveried Class 37 (coal sub-sector) No 37235 The Coal Merchants Association of Scotland on display at the Coalville depot open day on 11 June 1989.

And the abiding memory of the eighties must be of the greatest achievement, the enormous increase in passenger traffic. BR indeed continued to change the country's very geography, Gatwick suddenly becoming much closer to London with its Express every fifteen minutes, places like Peterborough and Swindon now almost as accessible as suburbs only fifteen miles away from Piccadilly. In the decade's final timetable, there is an express

20

Eastfield-allocated Class 37 No 37413 hauls the 09.50 Glasgow Queen St to Fort William near Achallader, approaching Rannoch Moor, on 29 September 1987. The rake is made up of early Mk2 and Mk1 coaches. The leading vehicle is open brake second (micro buffet) No 9107, one of eight converted from Mk2 BSOs during the 1980s.

One of the troublesome Leyland Class 155 units No 155302 forms a Provincial sprinter service, the 15.10 Portsmouth–Cardiff in July 1988. It is climbing the 1 in 75 of Ashley Hill bank, Bristol.

There is still much evidence of the traditional railway environment in this view of Whitby on 18 August 1982. A Metro-Cammell three-car dmu passes Bog Hall signalbox with semaphore signalling, redundant engine and goods sheds and a rather derelict goods yard (with full coal staiths) on leaving the station with the 09.15 Whitby–Darlington service.

APT-P unit No 370001 passes Lambrigg, north of Oxenholme, at 10.52 on 19 March 1986 with a high-speed test run between Crewe and Carlisle. Scrapping of the APT vehicles commenced a few months later.

every 15 minutes (plus one extra) between Swindon and Paddington over a two-and-a-half-hour period in the morning rush. Though the policy has been to raise the price of long-distance season tickets well above the average, for thousands there is still standing room only on the high-speed commute.

Despite the cost, many measure their distance from London in time, and corridors along the main lines north and west out of the capital compete very favourably with traditional Metroland and Southern electrified territory. Not that Network SouthEast's more everyday trains are short of patronage. The experts got their calculations wrong and the daily influx into London is vastly greater at the end than the start of the eighties, or any prediction forecast. Nor is it only an influx into London. More commuters actually go from London to Reading to work than vice versa. Swindon and Peterborough probably have more commuters going to them than their total everyday passenger traffic in the steam age. Many of the northern and Scottish cities also experience sharply enhanced rush hours. It is again the age of going to work by train.

The buoyant economy at the end of the eighties of course helped in part by increasing road congestion, forcing many to take the train who would have preferred to drive. This happens even in rural areas, such as between Exmouth and Exeter. Bus competition has been hampered not only by road congestion but upheaval in the road-passenger industry. Who a decade ago would have thought it possible that the chief benefactor of bus deregulation would be BR? That it is results from the chaotic competition and lack of liaison, hundreds of thousands of would-be passengers turning to the railway with its reliable timetable for want of proper information about road services.

That planning has been poor is more the fault of the economy than BR,

Peppercorn K1 2-6-0 No 2005 reflects the morning sun as it passes Boldon Colliery with the Northumbrian Mountain Pullman on 22 January 1983. This was a North Eastern Locomotive Preservation Group special (No 2005's owners) which included the SLOA Pullman rake.

the high interest rates at the end of 1989 being seen as likely to repeat the recession of 1981 out of which we climbed so painfully. Yet every year one questions the quality of many BR decisions. In 1989 we were assured there was no, absolutely no, case for electrifying between Edinburgh and Glasgow: a short trunk route between two major conurbations, electrification already in place at either end, that would seem to be the absolute classic next stage. But there never has been anything as sensible as a planned, rolling programme of electrification. The achievement of the eighties was that at least something was achieved out of the stops and goes. And on the whole achieved at less cost than earlier schemes – with less disruption, too, especially on the East Coast main line. So Bedford, Leeds, Norwich, Hastings, Weymouth, are added to the places from which you travel electric to London, perhaps not so bad a score for the decade. Even Paddington's platform ends were given supports for overhead electrification when the Lawn was extended to accommodate a shopping centre, leaving Marylebone as the only other London terminus yet to see electric activity. But even Marylebone sees a revitalised Chiltern service. (Amazing how quickly BR abandoned its scheme to close Marylebone when a scheme popped up to turn it into a kind of Victoria Coach Station for northern routes!)

Personal memories: of the larger knots of passengers at reopened Templecombe than at most other stations between Exeter and Salisbury, a route far busier and better served than ten years ago; but of travelling from Southampton to Newton Abbot via Westbury having dinner with a traveller from London to Crewkerne, the common Westbury–Taunton section way north of both passengers' direct line being attractive because of the faster pace of HSTs. Of the scandalous way in which the railway hotels were sold off and nine-tenths have deteriorated rapidly since. Of the way that stations such as Inverness still remarkably reflect their region's economy. Of the Persil soap powder offers that enabled two passengers to travel for the fare of one and of the utter complexity of offers and restrictions that taxed the ingenuity of many booking clerks and ticket collectors until the Blue (cheaper) and White (all Fridays and occasional other days) Savers were standardised as BR's on the whole highly successful marketing tool against coach competition. Of ancient multiple units that keep going well beyond their years, the bane of commuters but still offering forward views of stunning coastal and moorland scenery. Of quadrupled track being reduced to double, double to single, more blade ends and diamonds taken out, yet a highly complex system still remaining on a truly national scale. Of more money-making opportunities taken such as Settle & Carlisle regular trains hauled specially by freight locomotives and carrying more passengers than any service train probably since the war. Of splendidly smooth rides out of King's Cross and Paddington, sporty ones out of St Pancras on the HSTs, and nerve-racking, noisy ones with hunting bogies on ordinary stock out of Euston. Of days one was proud to be associated with railways and too many (still only a sprinkling but so devastatingly disrupting) that one swore always to take the car next time.

No 86427 The Industrial Society *and 87005* City of London *head south through the Lune Gorge with a Mossend–Severn Tunnel Junction steel coil train on 23 February 1988.*

Birmingham RC&W Co Class 104 unit No 104325, in the bizarre ScotRail 'mexican bean' livery, works the 09.55 Oban to Crianlarich service near Tyndrum Lower on 29 September 1987. Note the high-intensity headlamp fitted above the destination blind.

A version of LNER apple green was applied to No 47522 Doncaster Enterprise *during the 1980s. The locomotive is seen here passing Stonebridge, Durham working the 17.29 Heaton carriage sidings to York, with the stock for the York–Cardiff postal service, on 10 June 1988.*

GWR-liveried Class 50 No 50007 Sir Edward Elgar (*originally* Hercules, *renamed in 1984*) *hauls a NSE service, the 12.15 Waterloo to Salisbury, near Pirbright Junction on 29 July 1989.*

The 14.20 King's Cross–Leeds InterCity service pulls away from Wakefield Westgate on 25 April 1989 powered by Class 91 No 91008. Note the difference in profile between the Mk3 stock and the Mk4-styled locomotive.

This book aims to serve several purposes. It should provide quick reference on the important events and trends, including motive power, traffic, vehicles and safety, in the eighties. With its pictures as well as text contributed by a team of experts, it portrays a colourful decade in which hope was more rekindled than lost. Our wish is that it will enable you better to recall and enjoy your own memories. Might we indeed suggest adding a personal loose-leaf comment and photograph or two within your copy for posterity?

Finally, a few guideline wishes for the 1990s: undoubtedly, first, that the Channel Tunnel will be completed without undue delay and that a new high-speed route will rapidly follow through Kent; that under their new chairman, Robert Reid the second, from Shell, due to take his post in October 1990, BR will somehow regain a touch of personality, warmth, humanity, without losing their commercial edge; that the policy of providing new and cheaper-to-operate stock for secondary routes rather than handing down yesterday's worn-out express trains pays real dividends and prevents too much discussion of 'bustitution'; and that defensive theory will give way to common-sense pragmatism over matters such as the quality of the printed timetable and what really benefits the customer.

2
MEMORIES OF THE 1980s

CHAIRMAN Sir Peter Parker was doing his best, but the 1980s opened with much the same worries of insecurity over government policy, lack of investment, and working practices which harked back to the old company rules.

Although the new chairman Sir Robert Reid had his critics, at the decade's end it was clear that his method of management had produced decisive changes. A slimmer BR was more confident, easier to contemplate privatising. There was no longer just the promise of investment, but much of it in place. With a backbone of electrification, traffic rising and the prospect of the Channel Tunnel, everyone was talking about the railways.

1980. At first, it seemed that the antics of marine woodworms in the piling of Barmouth's 115 span timber bridge would rob the Cambrian coast of its railway, but BR surprisingly stumped up £500,000 for short-term repairs, and, after a seven-month closure, the line was back in business.

With hyper-inflation, BR started the year with a 20 per cent fares increase – despite furious cost-cutting.

There were increasing signs that the APT project was foundering. The introduction of the three pre-production prototypes into timetabled service was abandoned through 'a series of technical difficulties'. The submission for sixty production trains was postponed.

The Liverpool & Manchester's 150th was celebrated by a cavalcade of locomotives through Rainhill. Unlike the Shildon display five years earlier, diesels and electrics were included.

BR spoke of replacing Ribblehead viaduct on the Settle & Carlisle with a new earth embankment to reduce maintenance, not that the stone structure was unsafe.

1981. 'Deltic Mania' is not too strong a label to attach to the last full year of the locomotive flagships of the East Coast main line. Undoubtedly the most powerful, distinctive and popular design of the post-steam era, their final months on secondary workings produced a near manic enthusiasm that happily led to six of the fleet of twenty-two heading for preservation.

It may have been heralded as a strategic disaster, but the Manchester–Sheffield electric route via Woodhead tunnel slipped quietly into oblivion, due ceremony avoided because of the public puzzlement that a heavy freight route should be axed only twenty-five years after complete modernisation. The post-mortems continue but the truth is, that from an operational

West Coast up to date. Willesden-based Class 90 No 90006 (new 9 September 1988) climbs Shap at Greenholme with the 14.30 Euston–Glasgow service on 10 May 1989. Later InterCity examples received 'Mainline' livery.

Double-headed Class 37s Nos 37501 Teeside Steelmaster *and 37502* British Steel Teeside *haul the 10.47 British Steel Lackenby to Corby coil train through Cargo Fleet, Middlesbrough on 15 November 1988. Both locomotives were named at Thornaby in March 1987 when 37501 also received its 'British Steel' blue livery.*

Wessex Electric. A five-car Class 442 unit forms the 09.46 Poole and Bournemouth to Waterloo service passing through Pirbright, Surrey on 20 February 1989. The Basingstoke Canal runs parallel with the railway in the background.

Recently modified Class 47/8 (with extended-range fuel tanks) No 47818 heads a Holyhead to Carlisle charter train, Victoria Travel's Settle–Carlisle Express, through Baron Wood on 6 May 1989.

viewpoint, the 1,500V DC Woodhead line is not missed for a moment.

Unprintable were many of the comments when BR and Leyland collaborated on the ultimate basic DMU, slotting standard bus bodies on to coach frames, with an underbody power unit, and a flimsy cab bolted to each end. The seats were simple and uncomfortable, the noise intolerable, but it still shaped a disastrous decade of short-term economy stock building that is now being regretted.

1982. Millions of pounds of investment meant nothing to Bedford–St Pancras commuters when their long-awaited new electric trains were laid up in the sidings while BR and the rail unions hammered each other over one-man operation. It eventually saved a year's tyre wear on the Class 317s, and meant a lot more string and sticky tape on the clapped-out DMUs. Britain as a whole experienced thirty-four days of strikes.

We all feared the worst when BR withdrew InterCity services from the Settle & Carlisle. Stories started about the unsafe state of Ribblehead viaduct; it was another case of closure by stealth. Enter the campaigners.

The visit of Pope John Paul II over the Spring Bank Holiday returned people to the railways in numbers not seen since the 1950s. It was an enthusiast's delight as BR moved rolling stock from anywhere and everywhere to convey Papal followers to masses at Canterbury, York, Wembley, Coventry, Liverpool, Manchester, Glasgow, Edinburgh and Cardiff. That meant twelve-car DMU rakes, Sunday services on non-Sunday routes, and hosts of locomotive-hauled 'Popex' specials. As for his Holiness himself, he was treated to a ride from Gatwick to Victoria behind the Royal loco No 73142 *Broadlands* bearing the special Southern headcode 'HF' (Holy Father).

The adoption of the name ScotRail by the Scottish Region was far more than a marketing ploy. The new regular-interval timetable was actually understandable by the common man, the first real hint of a corporate localised identity, and the first appearance centre stage of one of the new breed of managers – Chris Green.

How unfortunate that the long-awaited arrival of comfortable Mark 3 sleeping coaches coincided with a downturn in the national economy. While the sleepers ran empty, BR picked up the hard-pressed nocturnal travellers with a new cheapo 'Nightrider' using spare first-class coaches with fluorescent lighting encased in soothing blue plastic.

It became possible to change trains again at the Welsh mining town of Blaenau Ffestiniog. Yes, the twenty-eight-year effort by the Festiniog to restore service to Blaenau Ffestiniog was finally completed, resulting in increased business on BR's branch from Llandudno Junction.

1983. They were building new railways across the world, but there had to be an extraordinary reason to do that in Britain. The fourteen miles of new main-line railway on the East Coast main line, bypassing Selby at a cost of £60 million, resulted from threat of coalmining subsidence under the old formation.

East Coast contrasts. Class 40 No 40124 hauling a Tyne Yard–Dringhouses, York vacuum-braked freight is overtaken by HST set No 254004 at Ouston Junction, Chester-le-Street on 16 May 1980. The HST rake includes two catering vehicles (TRSB and TRUK) and is made up to nine cars by the addition of a Trailer Second.

33

Class 50 locomotive No 50041 *Bulwark* arrived at Paddington station on its side! It had been derailed at the entrance while approaching at speed with a sleeper service from Penzance; miraculously there were no serious injuries, though much of the track at the station throat had to be relaid. As for *Bulwark*, it was severely damaged, but valuable enough to be repaired.

Orange and black meant Strathclyde, green and cream West Yorkshire, and yellow and white Tyne & Wear, as passenger transport executives provided public proof of their interest (and subsidy) of metropolitan rail services by applying their own liveries. As for the West Midlands, it tried various shades of red, white, blue, and grey and even canary yellow but by the end of 1989 had still not got its formula worked out.

The latest economy drive saw the introduction of a prototype bus-bodied hauled passenger coach, quickly labelled by journalists as 'third class'. They were right.

The arrival of the new Saturday 125mph High Speed Train service from Swansea to Pembroke provided a new job for the train guard: he had to leap out at Manorbier to open the crossing gates, wait for the train to clear the crossing, close them, and then walk seven coach lengths to give the driver the right away.

LNER *Flying Scotsman* became an old age pensioner in style with a series of runs over its old haunts from Peterborough to York. A pity so many kamikaze spectators chose to stand in the four foot to watch it go by.

Whoever would have thought it possible? Almost unnoticed, the standard vacuum-braked 12 ton freight van was eliminated. They were so ubiquitous that grounded bodies used as sheds will be a feature of Britain's farmyards for decades to come.

Surprise, surprise, the year ended with the news that BR wanted to close the Settle & Carlisle. The rescue machine was poised for action, and the rest is now history.

1984. Great news – the £306million electrification of the East Coast main line was approved in one go on 27 July.

A veritable flood of new locomotive liveries, some smart, some misguided and dreadful, transformed the station scene from a mass of standard blue and grey to an unpredictable display of sector showing off. The Western Region won the prizes however for its nostalgic application of lined GWR steam-style livery to five of its top-link diesels. Sir Edward Elgar would have been delighted.

The economist's Utopian dream of a rural railway without station staff, platelayers and expensive signalling staff came closer with the introduction of radio signalling over the Far North lines from Inverness. As BR discovered however, it is essential to give maintenance crews skiing lessons to cope with mountaintop transmitters in winter, and placate Irish TV viewers whose screens suddenly go fuzzy.

The Gatwick Express was a good demonstration of how to create maximum impact with the minimum of resources, simply recycled Mark 2 coaches, a rebuilt driving trailer from a scrap EMU, a spare Class 73 locomotive converted to push-pull, and a generous helping of new paint. The result: millions of contented passengers, and millions of extra revenue.

The late 1980s will be remembered by many for their tragic rail accidents, but 1984 witnessed the deliberate, spectacular and entertaining wrecking of Class 46 locomotive No 46009 to demonstrate that a nuclear flask is safe even when struck by a 100mph train. The £1.5million show by the CEGB also showed that Mark 1 coaches are remarkably resilient to high-speed impacts. However, eighteen people were killed during the year. Major incidents were at Wembley, Eccles, and Morpeth.

End of an era. No 55015 Tulyar having returned light engine from Edinburgh to York on 2 January 1982 became the last Deltic to be switched off by BR. The locomotive was subsequently acquired by the Deltic Preservation Society.

Goodbye LNER, farewell soon LMS. The replacement of the old electric units on the Manchester–Hadfield line and most of the Merseyrail network with second-hand BR sliding-door stock removed the last pre-Nationalisation trains. Happily, preservation groups stepped in to save some stock for posterity.

Despite all the publicity to the contrary, Trans-Pennine services moved through another Cinderella phase when the travelling public quickly rumbled that the 'new' locomotive-hauled services used rolling stock actually older than the DMUs they replaced. However, at least a new generation of diesel unit was in mind.

The 14.20 King's Cross to Edinburgh parcels train is stabled overnight at Newcastle Central station on New Year's Eve 1981. Motive power is provided by No 40092.

Steam made its last gasps in BR passenger trains, through the heating pipes of passenger coaches. There were enough new coaches at last to enable the steam-heat-only Mark 1 vehicles to be discarded, and enact new operating practices with newly converted electric heat, air-braked diesel locomotives. Even in Scotland.

Gresley 'A4' Pacifics were big news. No 4468 *Mallard* was being prepared for a return to steam for the 50th anniversary of its 1938 world record speed run. There were also delightful rumours that the heavy overhaul on sister No 4498 *Sir Nigel Gresley* would see it repainted green as No 60007. Wishful thinking. It reappeared in garter blue.

1985. The 150th anniversary of the founding of the Great Western was marked in style but to many it will be remembered for the decision to shut down Swindon Works.

Union leader Arthur Scargill's dream of political victory crumbled with the collapse of the national miners' strike. But it decimated BR's annual accounts, and ultimately the freight network, as the government then approved a severe pruning of unremunerative collieries. British Coal had its own Dr Beeching.

The West Country's joy at being able to combine quality and tradition in the shape of brand-new brown-and-cream-liveried bus-based four-wheeled diesel units for local branch services turned to dismay when their long wheel-base caused ear-splitting squeals on tight curves, and they had to be rapidly replaced by the thirty-year-old DMUs they had supplanted, fortunately not yet scrapped. Publicity machine called the units 'Skippers'. Locals called them 'Slippers'.

It was goodbye to the Class 40s. Fashions change, and the hulk-like diesels that were so unwelcome as steam replacements twenty-five years previously were given a massive send-off from the new generation of enthusiasts. On cold January nights, they camped out on platforms for the last experiences of 'Whistler' haulage, as the class of two hundred was whittled down to just one, the rebuilt, pioneer D200.

What was described as 'modular catering' or 'Cuisine 2000' was introduced on expresses out of Euston. The exotic land-prepared dishes did not go down well. Technology has not managed to replace the smell, taste and enjoyment of freshly cooked food, but some traditional cooking on board did survive.

1986. The thirty-year rundown of the Great Central Railway terminus at Marylebone (a prelude to seemingly inevitable total closure), was dramatically slammed into reverse gear on 30 April when BR admitted blossoming Chiltern Line services could not possibly be handled by Paddington, Euston, or even handed over to London Transport. The answer, was, investment and modernisation. A new film *Give My Regards to Broad Street* achieved extra significance on 30 September when all pleas for a reprieve were rejected, and the North London mausoleum closed its doors to passengers and awaited total demolition.

It was bad enough having to admit that the APT train project was a dead duck, but BR shot itself in the foot and provided the cynical national media with a field day by selling off some of the vehicles to a Sheffield scrapyard. The strict rules of disposing of redundant vehicles by public tender was forgotten for the rest of the stock, dismantled very much behind closed doors at Derby Works. By 1989 InterCity director Dr John Prideaux was reassuring his customers that it was wrong to regard the APT as a failure; it had indeed been a great design success!

Unfavourable train reliability statistics are easily shrugged off until one of your passengers is a VIP. Eyebrows were raised in high places in February when Class 47 locomotive No 47457 failed near Cambridge in charge of the Royal Train. Inside was none other than the Queen.

After his success in rebuilding morale in Scotland, Chris Green went for the big one – London. As the director of the new Network SouthEast, he never shied away from the divisive problems of pre-Grouping company loyalty and post-war neglect, and as a media lover soon became a star. To the commuter, the new red, white and blue house colours just had to represent a commitment to strive for quality. It did sound convincing.

The Yanks are coming! The entire railway freight business took note of Foster Yeoman's radical decision to buy its own fleet of locomotives off the shelf from an American builder. An unshackled BR first seemed keen to follow suit, but then took the safer political option of ordering its own replacement machines from a domestic supplier.

The 1 in 117 climb to Woodhead tunnel, past the empty Torside reservoir, is tackled by Class 76 locomotives Nos 76031 and 76033 with a train of MGR empties from Fiddlers Ferry to Wath on 7 September 1980.

1987. It was a big year for electrification. Norwich and Cambridge were reached; Clydeside's £85million showpiece was completed with the linking up of Largs and Ardrossan Harbour to the main Ayrshire system; and the Great Northern system was extended north to Huntingdon and Peterborough. Royston–Cambridge and Watford–St Albans fill-in schemes were also approved. But the government proved it was no pushover when ruling that the Far North line from Inverness to Wick/Thurso could not share the new road bridge over the Dornoch Firth. All pleas fell on deaf ears.

BR meanwhile accelerated its elimination of older locomotive types redundant through a reduction of trip workings and arrival of new designs. The net effect was the end of the Class 25 and 27, and a remarkable stack of over thirty asbestos-contaminated loco bodies piled high in Vic Berry's Leicester scrapyard as he struggled to cope with the influx.

The great 'volte face' came on 7 October when BR's chairman Sir Robert Reid officially opened (or re-opened?) Birmingham's Snow Hill station closed after the LMR took over the old Great Western's lines. The tape was broken at the tunnel's exit by *Isambard Kingdom Brunel* in green with GWR-type plates and name. Old Moor Street station closed and all trains previously running there now use the new station. Work started almost immediately in planning the replacement of tracks northwards to Smethwick and the line to Stourbridge, Worcester and Hereford. A new Act was prepared for placing before Parliament the inter-urban tramway link to Wolverhampton.

The organisers of the Basingstoke Open Day succeeded in assembling the largest collection of motive power types ever seen on BR. Present were (deep breath), Classes 20, 24, 25, 27, 31, 33, 35, 40, 44, 45, 46, 47, 50, 52, 55, 56, 58, 73, 77 and 86.

One of the reasons for the survival of the S&C into the 1980s had been its ability to handle diverted WCML trains; this continued despite the withdrawal of InterCity services in the winter 1982–3 timetable. No 47472 approaches Garsdale with the rerouted 08.30 Glasgow–Euston on 18 April 1982. Note the turntable (minus stockade), now installed on the Keighley & Worth Valley Railway.

39

One of the ubiquitous Metro-Cammell built-dmus (No 101339) leaves the fuelling point at Glasgow's Eastfield TMD on 29 May 1982. A quarter of the decade has passed with little visible sign of change.

Electrification continued apace during the decade with the major investment on the East Coast main line and in East Anglia. No 31246 heads an overhead mast foundation train between Haughley Junction and Stowmarket on 18 June 1984.

The year ended in tragedy. The night of 16 October saw some of the worst storms across the south of England for hundreds of years. Trees fell across tracks like dominoes, and barely had services begun to return three days later when a Central Wales line bridge collapsed while being traversed by a DMU. Four lost their lives.

The end of year deadline for eradication of asbestos-contaminated rolling stock, agreed many years ago between BR and the unions, was quietly and mutually forgotten when it was realised it was a long way from being achieved unless services were decimated.

Not BR, to be sure, but the showpiece Docklands Railway opened with its driverless trains.

1988. The year started with five regions, and ended with six. The newcomer was Anglia, to manage the area east of the GN main line which has the fastest-growing population in the UK.

It was there for all to see – BR became less of a corporate business, more an overlord for the sectors who were expected to find their own feet with or without government subsidy. Privatisation was now daily conversation.

London's rail system was transformed with the opening of the Snow Hill tunnel, providing a through link from Bedford to Brighton via King's Cross Midland and Blackfriars. What a difference!

January saw the inauguration of the Bournemouth–Weymouth electrification and three months later £16.4million was promised to convert the Portsmouth–Southampton route.

Enter the Class 91, the new breed of East Coast main-line electric locomotive. The prototype series of ten appeared from BREL Crewe Works with a collection of teething troubles, but were in regular passenger traffic to

Preparations started in 1984 to return No 4468 Mallard to full working order for the fiftieth anniversary of its record-breaking run in 1988. 1986 saw the locomotive's return to steam in original streamlined condition. It is seen here, in a now historic view of York station, waiting to depart with the Scarborough Spa Express on 9 July 1986.

Leeds by the end of the year. What happened to their Electra branding, by the way? Exit the Class 45 'Peaks', the last surviving locomotives built at Derby Works – and *Flying Scotsman* to Australia for a year's tour.

The Sprinter DMU, the saviour of Provincial, proved both a success and a disaster. The success was the Metro-Cammell Class 156, which helped create a new-style hourly Anglia–North West service and transform domestic Scottish and Welsh services. The headache was the Leyland Class 155, withdrawn after only a few months with doors that jammed open.

The bustle at London termini to load newspaper trains ended in July when BR terminated the contracts remaining after the previous year's transfer to road by News International and the Mirror Group.

For sale: a complete railway. BR issued a prospectus for the handing over of the entire Settle & Carlisle line to private enterprise. But there were no serious takers.

Cornwall became more of a standardised railway with the demise of the timber-bodied clay hood. In their place arrived 125 new BR-sponsored air-braked CDA hoppers.

Steam really did come to an end on BR when the state-owned narrow-gauge Vale of Rheidol was sold, not without tears, to the Brecon Mountain Railway. In the deal were three steam locomotives and a new interloper in the shape of a diesel.

The biggest, and most tragic, news event of the year was the 12 December Clapham disaster, discussed in detail elsewhere.

1989. With Clapham still in people's minds, public confidence in BR was shattered again on 4 March when two Saturday afternoon trains collided at Purley, killing six and injuring over eighty more. This time, it was driver error.

Still with disaster, swirling flood waters felled the River Ness bridge at Inverness, isolating the Kyle and Far North lines. Good news was the decision to build a replacement.

Not in my back yard! While the citizens of Amiens demonstrated in favour of the High Speed Line from Paris to the Channel Tunnel serving their city, the rural stockbrokers of Kent revolted against the idea of an equivalent new railway from the tunnel to London.

The Settle & Carlisle was reprieved in a shock statement issued on 11 April, a triumph for pressure groups and local authorities. BR made an immediate start on the backlog of maintenance, including repairs to Ribblehead viaduct.

Recognition that London's traffic problems are reaching seizure point came when BR announced schemes for two new cross-city links costing £2,000 million – links between Paddington and Liverpool Street, and from King's Cross/Euston to Victoria; plus a tube line from Hainault to Wimbledon via Chelsea and Hackney. (But the new tube was less sure of itself, and revised versions of it during the next few months whiplashed over the map of south London like a demented snake.)

BR disposed of its BREL engineering business to its management.

The rail unions staged a series of strikes over poor pay and BR insistence on an end to collective bargaining, and were somewhat surprised to find themselves with public sympathy despite many complete network shutdowns. To their dismay, however Britain did not seize up without trains.

Railfreight's new locomotive design made its debut. The British-built Brush Class 60 will number at least a hundred examples, all with evocative names.

We learned for the second time that old London Underground trains never die: they are sold for another quarter-century's work on the Isle of Wight. Like the 1920s stock before them, 1938-design vehicles were shipped over to the island to provide a moderately more comfortable service between Ryde and Shanklin. It was good fortune for BR to be able to pick up the 1938 survivors – only retained into the 1980s to bail out the Northern Line from a vast increase in traffic.

The introduction of InterCity's Nightrider service seems to have caused some difficulty in the publicity department. Late nights? The spelling of Milton Keynes and stopping would suggest so.

45

3
REGIONS, SECTORS
AND PTEs

Regions. At the start of the 1980s the British Railways business was still run by five regions: the Eastern, Western, Southern, London Midland, and Scottish. The whole of Great Britain was divided between them on a strictly geographical basis, and – subject to the general supervision of the British Railways Board and its chief officers in London – each region was completely responsible for the planning, working, and selling of all rail services in its area (except in the seven provincial centres where PTEs had been established). In other words, the regions were both production and marketing organisations. True, certain services for which duplication of provision would have been especially absurd (such as the Legal Department) were centrally provided. True also that property questions had already been separated off from the main business, to be handled by the British Rail Property Board (also on a regional basis, but with somewhat different geographical areas from those used by the operating regions). Nevertheless, essentially the regions ran the show.

This regional structure came about by accident rather than design. Even before the 1923 Grouping some companies were strongly territorial, and several had working arrangements with one another within one geographical area. The grouping formalised the situation by creating four essentially geographically based companies, even though they did stray into one another's territories. Nationalisation saw the basic pattern retained, although the Scottish elements of the London Midland & Scottish and the London & North Eastern Railways were hived off to form a Scottish Region, and the North East based on York also became a separate region.

Changes in the 1950s and early 1960s brought rationalised boundaries to create tighter geographical regions and eradicate penetrating lines and competition. So the Southern lost its lines west of Salisbury to the Western, the Western gave up its lines in the West Midlands to the London Midland, the Eastern surrendered its access to Manchester, and the London Midland gave up to the Eastern and North Eastern its Yorkshire lines.

Massive structures remained, many attitudes and management at the beginning of the decade were very similar to those of long ago. The regional general manager remained effectively the managing director of a large company. His chief officers formed a board which had a very considerable measure of authority to determine its own ways (witness, for example, the Western Region's adventure with diesel-hydraulic locomotives when the remainder of British Railways was following the diesel-electric path, or

Scottish Region. The extremely utilitarian front end of the Sprinters is displayed against the massive ironwork of the Forth Bridge by No 150284 as it heads south working the 13.40 Dundee to Edinburgh train on 29 August 1988.

47

the Eastern Region's policy of civil engineering for speed). An innovation in organisation sectorisation resulted in the regions losing their business roles and becoming purely the providers of services and facilities. Within the regions there have also been big changes, notably first the creation of area management, then the abolition of the divisions. The area manager is responsible for all aspects of the working railway in his patch, including operations, and his role in liaison with the sectors, which have only a limited presence away from headquarters, is crucial.

There must now be a real question-mark over the continuing existence of the regions. They have been downgraded in areas like Tyneside and Manchester by the creation of the PTEs. With sectorisation they have lost most of their planning, commercial, and marketing activities. Their function now is to make a good job of delivering the railway services that the PTEs and sectors want to buy from them. Is there any need in the future for an intermediate level between headquarters and the greatly enlarged areas? Is there indeed a case for some form of national track authority in place of six regions? Yet, long after the North East had lost its separate region, on 4 April 1988 East Anglia was given independence. Anglia controls East Anglia lines of Network SouthEast serving the London commuter area more locally than they were being controlled by the Eastern at York. Management where the job is actually being done may show the way forward in other ways, though the granting of extra power to Cornish Railways was a short-lived experiment. One thing is certain: further changes in the 1990s will reflect the role of the railway as a business out there in a hard, competitive world. The 1980s have been a period of considerable and long-overdue change.

PTEs. All the present PTEs were already firmly established by the start of the 1980s, and they have survived the 1986 abolition of the metropolitan councils. Their creation limited the powers of the Scottish, Eastern, and London Midland Regions in a number of major conurbations outside London. The Western and Southern Regions have no PTEs in their areas.

The principal change in the 1980s has come with the creation of the sectors, in that the PTEs primarily talk business to the sectors these days, the region then delivering the agreed product. The PTE decides on frequency, and it can even specify – within reason – the timings of the trains it wants. It considers whether it wishes to invest further in rail, simply keep the rail services it has, replace rail with bus, or seek other solutions to local transport problems. It sets fare levels. (All the PTEs have done a great deal of work on the integration and simplification of fare-structures and the provision of interchangeable tickets.) It can even buy rolling stock, and several PTEs have made extensive purchases of the new 1980s multiple-units. Strathclyde and West Yorkshire, for example, both have their own Super Sprinters. All have sponsored rail investment in one form or another and are continuing to do so. Tyneside has its Metro, Liverpool its underground lines, Strathclyde a lavish electric system. Manchester at first lost out very badly on rail investment, but now it has some compensation in the Windsor Link and is

going ahead with an advanced tram system that will take over a number of heavy rail routes. Birmingham and Sheffield are making similar plans. West Yorkshire, having presided over a massive expansion of rail traffic in recent years, is pushing for more electrification in the wake of the successful completion of InterCity's electrification to Leeds.

With the abolition of the metropolitan councils in 1986, responsibility for the supervision of the PTEs has passed to joint boards of delegates from each of the metropolitan boroughs. Since they have lost their buses through bus deregulation they have become essentially planning and co-ordinating bodies for both rail and road modes. So far, many of the improvements they brought about have survived, and the fragmented bus industry has not yet led to a breakdown of the integrated ticketing that marked such a step forward in British practice.

Sectors. Sectors are of course the most significant creation of the 1980s. In

Anglian memories. Class 47 No 47580 County of Essex *pulls away from the elegant Norwich Thorpe station with the 15.20 to Liverpool Street on 22 June 1984.*

49

Invaluable service. Severe winter weather conditions create much hardship for the isolated communities along the Settle–Carlisle line and the railway provides the only reliable form of transport at such times. No 31410 leaves Blea Moor tunnel with the 08.57 Leeds–Carlisle train on 5 February 1983.

the mid 1970s there was an abortive attempt to develop a new way of managing the industry in the Territories Plan (which would have given a structure very similar to that developed in Germany in much earlier years and still in use both on DB and DR), but this failed largely on account of union opposition. Each territory would have been a complete business organisation in its own area, but because no territory would have been large enough to run a complete main line a great deal more co-operation would have been necessary than existed between the regions, and on a much more formal basis.

The basis for a different type of approach already existed. Dr Beeching had drawn attention to the shortcomings of the railway's accounting practices. Slowly better systems were introduced, making it possible to look more analytically at what was happening. This made it possible to group together different types of service (InterCity's identity was first established on this basis) and look at their costs and revenues in a sensible manner. The whole process was greatly helped by the much more widespread availability of computers. And the remit of the railways was changed. Government decided

Cardiff-based single-car unit No 55032 carrying the dragon and red 'V' of Provincial's Welsh 'Valley Lines' is seen near Porth at the head of a Barry Island to Treherbert train on 15 August 1985.

Two-car diesel parcels unit (Nos 55972 and 55982) passes the fine North Staffordshire 'Jacobean' gables of Stone station en route to Birmingham. These Class 127 units were modified (for Parcels sector use) after their eventual replacement by emus on the St Pancras–Bedford route.

that the whole of the railway freight business should pay its way. Then a policy directive in 1977 reinforced by the new government in 1979, also insisted that InterCity should run commercially even if other parts of the passenger business were to receive grant-aid under the 1968 Act.

Under the chairmanship of Sir Peter Parker the concept of the commercial railway and the social railway was developed at the end of the 1970s and the start of the 1980s. The first was to be run on strictly business lines, while the second needed financial support. This emphasised not only the importance of the distinct types of business but the difference between the businesses and the operations.

So on 4 January 1982 the railway's commercial undertaking was divided into its separate elements. Freight and parcels had always been seen as distinct entities, and these naturally formed two of the new sectors. On the passenger side InterCity was taken out first; then all the London-commuter-belt services were grouped to form London & South East (later renamed Network SouthEast); finally, everything left over formed Other Provincial Services (later renamed Provincial). The last two were the social railway, requiring continuing support in grant-aid for the provision of socially essential services in the capital, in the great conurbations, and in rural areas.

British Rail's accounts have charted financial progress. InterCity turned in its first profit in 1988–9, only a year after transitional support was withdrawn. Network SouthEast has improved its performance beyond what anyone could have dreamed might be possible. And now that Provincial has sorted out its rag-bag inheritance into clear service-groups, it too can show great steps forward in many areas.

There is a need for close and on-going liaison with the regions and PTEs, but at the end of the day it is the sector that calls the tune. Each sector director looks at his business on a national level, ignoring regional boundaries, and has the power to deploy all his resources to the best commercial advantage. The best example of this has been the deployment of the HST fleet. This was first bought in the 1970s by the regions, but it has been deployed under sectorisation with singleminded determination to maximise earnings. Yet while InterCity is supposed to be one business, offering consistent standards throughout Britain, many regional differences in what the traveller actually experiences die slowly.

It is now the sectors which sponsor investment in track and signalling as well as rolling stock, that must deal with the modernisation of stations, and so on. The decisions are commercial: what will earn the best return on the investment? Questions that should have been asked long ago are now being asked – and, more importantly, answered. In years to come the commercialisation of BR via sectorisation could well be seen by historians as important as grouping and nationalisation.

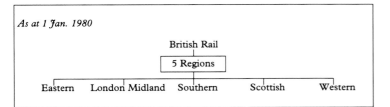

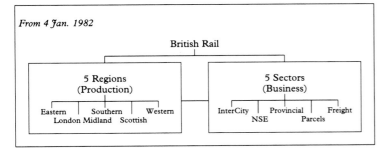

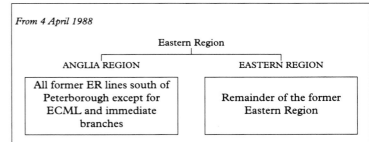

4
EXPRESSES EVER FASTER

THE 1980s will be remembered as the decade in which far-reaching changes were initiated on Britain's InterCity network. But at its start there were two great threats: the economic recession and the Thatcher Government's attitude to nationalised industry spending limits and investment criteria.

Despite the immediate success of the new fleet of 125mph trains which brought new standards of safety and on-board comfort firstly on the Western Region services out of London (Paddington) and then on the East Coast main line from London (King's Cross), so much of what had been gained in the late 1970s was lost as the economic recession started to bite. The impact was twofold. The sharp decline in business activity severely reduced the volume of full-fare first-class ticket sales while the increase in unemployment and interest rates curtailed to a drastic degree levels of disposable income available for leisure purposes such as optional standard-class rail journeys. This loss of optional travel was also exacerbated by the intensified competition from long-distance coaches following the liberalisation of route licensing in the 1980 Transport Act. Given the choice in such circumstances, many of InterCity's customers on low or fixed incomes – in particular students and senior citizens – preferred the cheaper but slower coach option.

Faced with such a quick and potentially damaging erosion of its business base, BR tackled the situation on two fronts – reduction of costs and a head-on response to the coach operators with bargain fare offers.

A 10 per cent cut in loaded train miles was phased between June 1981 and October 1982. Skilfully applied, these cuts were made in such a way as to protect the sectors' long-term business-base stability. With relatively little loss of traffic or even complaints, InterCity was able to phase out many of its old life-expired Mk 1 coaches.

Meeting the coach competition necessitated a more risky strategy: head-on confrontation at the low-price end of the market. By introducing bargain-level fares – 'Savers' – BR's aim was to generate sufficient extra passengers to achieve a net revenue gain. The tactics succeeded and the erosion of optional business was stopped. Train loadings were increased and unit costs reduced. It was the creation of the bargain-priced Saver which paved the way for an airline-style market segmentation which has subsequently played such an important part in InterCity's move into profit which was achieved towards the end of the decade.

The first indications of the new 1979 Conservative Government's attitude to investment became apparent when BR sought approval to build an

Mk4 DVT No 82203 with Mk4 stock and No 91009 providing rear power race through Potters Bar on 4 November 1989 on a proving run prior to entering service.

additional seven HST sets to cope with the first flush of growth following the launch of 125mph services on the East Coast main line the previous year. After much haggling, approval was only obtained for those four out of the seven sets which could meet the much higher rate of return which would henceforth be applied to BR investment. If BR could not make a case for seven trains for one of its most profitable routes, it was clear that plans for a second tranche of HSTs for the Cross Country group of services would not satisfy the new criteria. These were the circumstances which led BR to terminate HST building with a fleet of ninety-five operational trains. It is a matter of history that as the 1980s drew to a close, a few extra HSTs to cope with the unprecedented levels of business by now on offer would have been very welcome.

Running a national business as complicated as a railway network is in all circumstances a daunting task, but the challenge is even more difficult when the government of the day can effectively veto any major decision. For the past forty or so years since the railways passed into public ownership, the issue of social support – that is the extent to which unremunerative routes should be directly subsidised by the taxpayer – has never been entirely clear. For

Beginning of the decade on the WCML. No 86247 (named Abraham Darby *in 1981) speeds through the Lune Gorge with an up 'Electric Scot' service on 22 March 1980. The train make-up is typical of the time with air-conditioned Mk2 stock supported by Mk1 catering and full brake coaches.*

Discontinued ECML sleeper service The Night Scotsman, 23.20 King's Cross to Edinburgh, is hauled north at Burnmouth behind No 47525 on 23 July 1983. The train was running approximately two hours late due to a broken rail at Northallerton. Note the Motor Rail vans at the rear.

example, in 1976 a White Paper on transport policy issued by the then Labour Government, stated that inter-urban passenger transport in Britain should not be subsidised. Unequivocal though that statement was, it was not until the 1979 Conservative Government got into its stride that this tenet was raised from aspirational status to a specific directive that InterCity must operate as a self-financing business.

How to cope with the separate issues of the economic recession, the need for major investment such as the electrification of the East Coast main line and identification of those parts of the network or services which needed direct government subsidy, was the overriding concern of the BR Board at the start of the 1980s. However, it was not the complexity of issues per se that was the problem. It was more a matter of how BR's organisation should be adapted to cope with a much tighter (but more specific) set of government directives.

The story of how the traditional management through the regions has been transformed into a marketing one based on the sectors is told elsewhere.

So far as InterCity is concerned sector management has brought two major benefits: overall responsibility for deployment of its rolling stock fleet, and the building of a national range of express train products. The first example of equipment redeployment came in 1982 when the then director (Cyril Bleasdale), faced with a serious downturn on Great Western sub-sector services out of Paddington, decided to move ten HSTs to the Midland main line so that a badly needed improvement could be implemented on this potentially profitable and much neglected route. Under the previous organisation it would have taken months of internal wrangling to resolve the conflicting aspirations of regionally based management. Transfer of all Anglo-Scottish sleeping car services from the East to the West Coast main line from May 1988 was a similar decision based on a corporate rather than a regional viewpoint.

An important feature of the 1980s which has contributed to InterCity's financial turnround is market segmentation and pricing – or the shaping of products to meet the needs of customer groupings. Essentially this concept is not new – from the early days our railways were providing first-, second- and even third-class accommodation and the excursion ticket was quickly used to sell spare capacity. What is new is the much greater degree of sophistication which is now necessary to produce the maximum revenue yield from each and every InterCity journey. Today's equipment – trains and track – is very expensive to provide and maintain; to cover its basic costs it has to be in service providing revenue for up to say sixteen hours per day. But, as we know, demand for seats is not evenly spread. Monday-to-Friday peak-hour trains – the 07.25 from Manchester to Euston and the 16.30 back to Manchester are cases in point – will always load well, but the stock providing these two services will also make two midday trips for which custom may be sparse. Market segmentation and pricing has provided the answer.

InterCity now has a range of offers – first class, standard and the Saver ticket – the purpose of which is, by offering varying fares to channel demand

The corporate identity image has been slow to disappear, with the old standard liveries lingering even on InterCity services. Here No 50034 Furious, which has subsequently been painted in NSE livery, heads the 13.40 Paddington to Penzance train under Taunton's west signal gantry on 11 April 1986. The GWR semaphores were replaced a few weeks after this, losing the character of a much older 'corporate identity'.

so that it can spread the load over existing capacity. To many it has complicated the process of selling InterCity travel, but – like the airlines who face similar problems – it is a necessary tool to maximise the earning potential of high-cost equipment.

By the second half of the 1980s InterCity was well on its way towards self-sufficiency and genuine operating profits. A greatly reduced fleet of locomotives and coaches along with better overall control and increased patronage (especially in long-distance commuting) resulted in a sharp recovery. In 1984–5 the sector returned a loss of £157million; in one of the most dramatic business turnrounds in recent years this has become a £24million profit in 1988–9. From such an unpromising start in 1980, BR has become the first railway in the world to provide a long-distance passenger-railway service without subsidy.

West Coast Main Line. One of the ironies of the 1980s is that while the East Coast main line started to take delivery of its second-generation 125mph equipment, the maximum speed of West Coast trains had only moved from 100 to 110mph.

This sorry state of affairs follows from the failure of the Advanced Passenger Train (APT) prototype to achieve sufficient reliability to justify the ordering of an operational fleet which could exploit the 'tilting' train concept on BR's long-haul routes.

Space precludes a full account of the APT saga, but briefly stated the purpose of the tilting train is to run through speed-restricted curves in complete safety and without loss of passenger comfort at much higher speeds than can be achieved with conventional rolling stock, enabling journey times to be reduced without recourse to realigning and upgrading existing tracks at prohibitive cost.

As BR looked towards the 1970s and into the 1980s, it was realised that if InterCity was to survive the growing threat posed by the airlines and the rapid extension of motorways, train speeds would have to be lifted beyond the prevailing norm of 80mph start-to-stop between main business centres. While a good proportion of the West Coast route could be raised from 100 to 125mph at reasonable cost, there are many locations where it is necessary to impose speed restrictions because of curvature and track geometry. As the APT was so ideally suited to the needs of the West Coast main line and offered the possibility of major train service improvements, BR – regrettably as matters transpired – became wedded to the project to the extent that no other traction possibility was considered. It is now a matter of history that – notwithstanding an outlay of £150million at current prices on research and development and prototype trains – the technical potential of the train was never achieved and in 1983 the entire project was abandoned.

Had BR had more time and more funding, had the government been more sympathetic towards the railway investment and had there been no recession, the APT might have eventually been successful – but that is another story. (By 1988 the Italian Railways had produced a tilting train – the Pendolino – which

An aerial view of the approaches to Liverpool St station on 4 February 1989. Passing Class 86/2s Nos 86242 James Kennedy *and 86221* BBC Look East, *which are stabled prior to hauling one of the hourly InterCity services to Norwich, is Class 315 emu No 315850 forming the 11.42 from Southend Victoria.*

appears to be successful.) Not only was the non-fulfilment of the APT an enormous financial loss but since its rapid adoption in 'squadron service' had been presumed there were no alternative plans for either trains or track.

As the depression began to affect West Coast loadings it soon became clear that it was no longer possible to sustain the level of service provided in the 1974 Glasgow electric timetable. The hourly off-peak service from Euston to Liverpool and Manchester was an early casualty when the service was cut back to a ninety-minute headway, but the most far-reaching change concerned the Anglo-Scottish services between Euston and Glasgow. Historically, Scotland was always perceived as the premier West Coast market on which the case for electrification from Weaver Junction to Glasgow (Motherwell) was made. But by 1985 the sad reality had to be faced that – so far as InterCity was concerned – the market had changed, probably for ever. Business people – no longer prepared to spend five hours or more on a daytime Euston–Glasgow journey – had switched to air, while leisure travellers had been lured away by the bargain-priced coaches. To offset the loss of Glasgow business, extra stops were added to the daytime service which was revamped to serve towns such as Warrington, Wigan, Lancaster, Oxenholme and Penrith which offered greater business prospects. Only the *Royal Scot* remained as a viable Euston–Glasgow train but with a schedule fifteen minutes slower than the five-hour norm established in the 1974 timetable. At one stage the average time of the five daytime trains between Euston and Glasgow was over five and a half hours.

However the long-term decline of the West Coast main line was not a prospect that InterCity was prepared to accept. As a first stage towards

The May 1986 timetable saw the introduction of a new cross-London service from North West England to the South East. On the second day of the new service, 13 May 1986, No 47446 arrives at Kensington Olympia with the 17.45 Dover to Manchester train. The trains to Brighton over this route brought echoes of the old Sunny South Express.

reviving the route's viability plans were made to accelerate certain key Glasgow services by raising the line speeds from 100 to 110mph; the second stage was to prepare an investment case for new equipment to fill the gap which would otherwise have been covered by APT.

Raising the maximum speed from 100 to 110mph was relatively easy. While the fleet of Class 87 locomotives and Mk 3 stock was capable of 110mph, the only guards' vans on the route were old Mk 1 cars restricted to 100mph. An agreement was obtained to run a small dedicated number of these at the higher speed. Broadly speaking the curvature and signalling on most of the 100mph sections were also fit for 110mph. The only added cost was the need for a second driver when running in excess of 100mph, but this was subsequently rescinded to 110mph.

Two 110mph trains in each direction were introduced from May 1984 and the entire service was upgraded in the following year. Subsequently, while the total number of 110mph trains was retained some were withdrawn from the Glasgow service in favour of key Manchester and Liverpool business trains.

In some respects the long-awaited authority for new West Coast locomotives proved to be something of a disappointment. Instead of the 125mph Class 89 prototype, an order was placed in January 1986 for twenty-nine Class 90 locomotives but they only have a potential of 110mph. To go with the new Class 90s an order was placed for twenty-nine Driving Van Trailers (DVTs) to replace the old Mk 1 guards' vans.

By the close of the 1980s the West Coast had started to regain some of its old vitality and was emerging as the most utilised and profitable part of the

Class 73 Electro-Diesel No 73120 leaves Gatwick propelling the 15.50 Express service to Victoria on 22 September 1986. Horley station is in the background.

InterCity network. Although no plans exist at present for 125mph train speeds, a more general extension of 110mph services is likely to start in 1990.

East Coast Main Line. Probably because it started the 1980s with a fleet of new 125mph HSTs which had made a major impact on its market, the East Coast main line was far better placed to withstand the rigours of the recession than its West Coast neighbour. While train mileage cuts were implemented in 1980/1, these were mainly marginal services covered by 100mph diesel-hauled trains the loss of which was of little long-term consequence. Indeed, for a time it enabled the service to become an all HST operation so that some places actually had a better service.

There were four major East Coast developments in the 1980s: the significant increase in HST productivity so that sets could be more extensively deployed to provide service to Inverness, Glasgow Queen Street, Hull and Cleethorpes; electrification of the route from Hitchin to Leeds with only minor interference to train services; introduction of a new track-maintenance strategy and transfer of overnight Anglo-Scottish sleeping-car services to the West Coast main line.

Although the original HST plans provided for two daily return journeys between King's Cross and Aberdeen, by judicious programming of the sets (plus some extra sets transferred from the Western region) it was possible to add on some extra trips to existing rosters. This enabled InterCity to introduce additional HSTs to Aberdeen, a pair of business services to Hull and Cleethorpes and an entirely new service *The Highland Chieftain* between King's Cross and Inverness with a journey time of seven hours.

Because of the need to refuel the two power cars, the practical operating range of an HST set is about 1,100 miles after which the unit must visit the depot to replenish its tanks. Needless to say such a constraint does not apply with electric locomotives. For several years BR had been trying to persuade the government to authorise the East Coast main line electrification; after considerable discussion this was eventually agreed in July 1984. The cost is £302million. The project entailed wiring from Hitchin to Leeds, Newcastle and Edinburgh, a total of 400 route miles. To work the new service a fleet of thirty-one Class 91 140mph locomotives and matching set of Mk 4 stock have been ordered. Intensive road testing of the first ten Class 91s started in the spring of 1988 and the first public services with the new Mk 4 stock started between King's Cross and Leeds in October 1989. Electric service at Edinburgh will start in May 1991. The fastest time between King's Cross and Edinburgh by HST in the 1980s was 4 hours and 23 minutes, with one stop at Newcastle; this will be cut to 4 hours from May 1991.

In mainland Europe the spacing between tracks and reversible signalling enables engineers to work on one track in complete safety while traffic continues to pass on the other. Here the engineers have to carry out most of their work on Sundays when traffic is light, but this often entails diversions and extended journey times followed by temporary speed restrictions for a few further days at the beginning of each week. To compensate for these temporary speed restrictions additional 'recovery' time is added to daytime schedules. Following studies by Eastern Region's engineers, a new track-laying strategy was introduced in 1987 whereby – with the use of a new machine called the Dynamic Track Stabiliser – tracks could be handed back by 06.00 on Monday morning at the full 125mph line speed, eliminating the need for a temporary speed restriction and associated recovery time allowance. Removal of these recovery allowances made possible a general acceleration of East Coast 125mph services from May 1987.

Overnight services for sleeping cars are a long-standing feature of BR's Anglo-Scottish routes, but this market has also changed. With a much smaller baseload of night traffic it was no longer viable to retain separate services to Scotland on both the East and West Coast routes. With the exception of the Newcastle service which was withdrawn, all East Coast Anglo-Scottish overnight services were transferred to the West Coast route from May 1988, making substantial economies.

Great Western. As was the case with the West Coast main line, the Great Western sub-sector was also badly affected by recession, but the decline at the start of the decade was matched by a spectacular recovery which started from the second half of the 1980s. The strength of the recovery was such that the Great Western was the first part of InterCity to move into profit.

It was the service between Paddington, Bristol and South Wales which felt the full impact of the recession. Things were made tougher by the completion of the M4 paralleling Brunel's main line to the Bristol area and across the Severn Bridge to Newport and Cardiff. It was perfect for low-fare express coach services. Loss of passengers led to dramatic train service cuts, enabling the sub-sector to release seven HSTs for the Midland main line.

Fortunately not only did growth return but on a scale far exceeding expectations. This was partly due to the economy's revival, but a major factor was the growth of long-distance commuting. With 125mph trains it was now possible to travel from places like Swindon, where house prices were lower, to London in less than an hour. Between 1985–6 journeys from Swindon to Paddington increased by 16 per cent, from Bath to Paddington by 12 per cent and from Bristol to Paddington by 20 per cent. By 1988 the morning-peak load was such as to necessitate a fifteen-minute clockface interval service from Swindon to Paddington between 06.30 and 09.00; additionally two services passed through Swindon without stopping.

To cope with its new level of business the Great Western has a fleet of thirty-one supplemented by some sets of locomotive-hauled stock. In 1988/9 unit availability had risen by 87 per cent and the average daily miles per operational set was 844. Originally the Great Western HST fleet consisted of 2 + 7 (two power cars with seven trailers) but in 1983 ten sets were given an additional trailer to work on the West of England line and to cover the prime business services. By May 1990 – after delivery of the first ten sets of the new Mk 4 stock for the East Coast main line – the Great Western will receive an additional HST set and sufficient trailers to make all HST formations 2 + 8.

Midland Main Line. Despite its importance as a trunk route linking London with Leicester, Nottingham, Derby, Chesterfield and Sheffield, until 1982 the Midland had Cinderella status. While it had received some decent Mk 2 air-conditioned stock, the maximum speed of its fleet of diesel locomotives was 90/95mph; average city-to-city speeds compared unfavourably with other parts of the InterCity network, and initially BR replied to local pleas that HSTs could not provide the answer, implying stagnation until perhaps the route was electrified and received APTs that could take the curvatures in their stride. However, when some of the Great Western HST sets became surplus to requirements an obvious option for redeployment was the Midland.

Although the curvature and track geometry precludes speeds much in excess of 100mph (except by upgrading at unacceptable costs) the power: weight ratio, acceleration and braking of the HSTs immediately demonstrated their worth and have made it possible to introduce some very useful cuts in journey times. A package of accelerations, improved peak-hour services and upgrading of the *Master Cutler* to Pullman status has generated new business.

To provide some much-needed improvement the InterCity director decided to transfer ten HSTs to the Midland – five from the Great Western, two from the East Coast main line plus three which were part of the build for the Cross Country (North East–South West) routes. A completely new Midland timetable was introduced in two stages in October 1982 and May 1983.

By the end of the decade, the Midland's outlook had been transformed. In 1990 it is planned to introduce a new Pullman service from Nottingham, an hourly off-peak service to both Nottingham and Sheffield and, by upgrading certain sections of the route for 110mph, a further general acceleration of all trains – unthinkable at the decade's start.

While the Midland main line is now a fully fledged HST route, it does not have its own depot. Its HSTs are provided from a combined pool of trains based at Neville Hill Depot (Leeds) used for both the Midland and East Coast main line services.

Cross Country. Comprising originally the North East/North West to South West/South East network of trains which were routed to run through Birmingham New Street (where they made a series of interchanges) the Cross Country InterCity sub-sector is now responsible for all services which do not use a London terminus. At one stage the Birmingham New Street interchange was an integral part of the West Coast electrified service and was based on an hourly sequence of arrivals/departures from the LMR electrified area and to the North East via Sheffield. As well as the series of long-distance trains which still run through Birmingham, the sub-sector now includes those few trains from the North West to Dover which run through Kensington Olympia in London, and the service between Manchester and Scotland via Preston and the West Coast main line.

In the late 1970s plans were prepared for a fleet of HSTs to operate the North East–South West (Newcastle/Leeds–Cardiff/Plymouth) route and these were introduced from 1982. As already mentioned, many plans had to be changed in the light of the recession and these included reduction of the number of Cross Country HSTs. Plans to upgrade parts of Cross Country routes for higher speeds were also deferred. However, although the Cross Country route has not emerged as a high-speed line per se, it now features a number of useful long-distance trains mainly aimed at the leisure market. They make some of the longest journeys on the BR network. Examples include the *Wessex Scot* (Glasgow/Edinburgh–Poole), the *Devon Scot* (Aberdeen/Glasgow–Plymouth) and the *Sussex Scot* (Glasgow/Edinburgh–Brighton) and there is also – an entirely new innovation – an overnight sleeping-car service between Poole and Glasgow, linking with the Plymouth–Edinburgh/Glasgow sleeper at Birmingham. All of these services are electrically hauled between Glasgow (Carstairs in the case of the Edinburgh trains) and Birmingham New Street where diesel locomotives take over.

One of the innovations of the decade, introduced in 1987, is the series of cross-country trains from the North West to the South Coast via Kensington Olympia. Not particularly successful, their number has been reduced. In 1989 came the opening of the Windsor Link connection in the Manchester area. This short section of the new railway has enabled through running from Preston and Bolton to Manchester Oxford Road and the through platforms at Manchester Piccadilly. Four daily InterCity services in each direction now take this route.

Anglia. After many years of indecision, in December 1981 BR obtained approval for the electrification of the main line from Colchester to Ipswich and Norwich and also the Harwich branch. The project was completed in May 1987, bringing new life both to the railway and the region it serves. There has been a particularly sharp increase in long-distance commuting. The Anglia services are worked by Class 86 locomotives and long rakes of Mk 2 air-conditioned stock.

Gatwick. Finally, the Gatwick Express service between London (Victoria) and Gatwick Airport was launched by InterCity in May 1984 and has been a great success. Introduction of the project followed a major upgrading of the tracks in the Croydon area and new signalling permitting 90mph speeds. The trains, running non stop every fifteen minutes, were formed from Mk 2 air-conditioned coaches made available following the changeover to HST operations on the Midland main line; the locomotives are Class 73s. The superior quality of the trains as well as their speed has both created new commuter business and extracted some traffic from the EMU service.

5
SPECIAL AND CHARTER TRAINS

IN the glass-enclosed rear section of the elegantly furnished 1892 Caledonian Railway observation car, the guests on the *Royal Scotsman* gathered to sip pre-dinner cocktails, nibble fresh foie gras canapés, and engage in polite rapport about their day's visit to Achnacarry Castle, the stately home of Sir Donald and Lady Cameron of Lochiel. In the growing queue for the buffet on the *Cheshire Cheese*, the passengers moved one place nearer the long-awaited ham and tomato sandwich in stony silence. If anyone spoke, it was usually only to voice condemnation of British Rail for the time it took to get served.

These were the opposite ends of the British special-train scene of the 1980s,

Black Five duo. No 4767 George Stephenson and No 5407 double head the Cumbrian Mountain Express over the S&C viaduct at Smardale, near Kirkby Stephen in April 1981.

Old Style Charter Train. An enthusiasts' railtour, The Thames Clyde Express commemorative special, St Pancras-Glasgow, approaches Garsdale on 19 February 1983 behind No 45117.

on either side of a conscious divide where the key words were price and profit. Six days of luxury on the *Royal Scotsman* (which included some steam haulage and as many glasses of Domaine des Berthiers as the liver would stand) at the end of the decade meant writing a cheque for £2,880. For the afternoon round trip from Crewe via Chester and Shrewsbury on the steam-hauled *Cheshire Cheese* (buy your own coffee), fifteen pounds was seeing you home and dry. The illustration shows how the special-train business developed in these ten years. In 1980, luxury trains like the *Royal Scotsman* and the *Venice Simplon Orient Express* did not exist. In 1989 they accounted for more than a quarter of BR's total charter-train revenue – and the trend is ever upwards.

In the 1970s the word was excursion, even then hardly fashionable, conveying an image of day trips to Blackpool and kiss-me-quick hats, of FA Cup tie specials (when football supporters swung rattles instead of knives), and of the classical BR Sunday Mystery Tour, when for ten and sixpence, you could be pretty certain of finishing up at Barry Island (again). The age of the bucket-and-spade seaside special was all but dead by 1980, so what filled the void? In the absence of any corporate direction, BR's excursion trains then were not much more than a mishmash of bright and not so bright ideas by divisional and area managers, which lost as much money as they made. Pied Piper and Merrymaker outings, locally organised specials, and a profusion of enthusiast-orientated railtours were run with little or no co-ordination between the regions, with the result that there was remarkable disparity in standards and even the level of fares.

It was not until sectorisation in 1983 and the creation by the then InterCity director Cyril Bleasdale of a special department to co-ordinate and develop charter-train operation, that BR began to get its act together. The man Bleasdale picked to head up its new Charter Train Unit was David Ward, who since 1976 had been responsible for co-ordinating main-line steam operations in conjunction with the Steam Locomotive Owners Association (SLOA). One of the unit's first initiatives was to commission the London Business School to undertake detailed research into BR's existing excursion business. The LBS report was uncompromising; it showed that even with full trains, there was little or no money at the bottom end of the market, whereas with first-class and full-dining trains, there was considerable profit potential. So the man on the street ceased to be the prime target of charter-train salesmen. Specials organised by InterCity became geared towards smaller numbers of passengers paying premium fares for VIP treatment in Pullman standard coaches with catering of comparable quality.

Under the old regional arrangements, the entrepreneurial independent tour organisers had been able to profit handsomely; especially those who catered for the insatiable demand by railway enthusiasts to travel 'new' lines behind favourite or unusual diesel types. Now there were hard times. Only operators able to fill their trains could expect to make a reasonable profit. Traditionally operators with insufficient passengers simply cancelled; BR now insisted that 10 per cent of the train hire charge – in some cases as much as £500 – be paid as a non-returnable deposit.

Since previously only about one in three advertised charter trains actually ran (there were indeed up to a hundred independent rail tour operators), the new regime immediately brought a crop of casualties, including in 1985 the Rail Tour Operators Association, the very organisation which had been established at Ward's insistence to negotiate train hire on behalf of all independents. (It must be said that the RTOA also contributed to its own downfall, by failing to get a grip on in-fighting among its own members.)

Another development during the first half of the 1980s hastened the decline in ordinary charter-train operation: the wholesale withdrawal of ageing steam-heated 90mph Mk 1 coaching stock from which such trains were usually formed. The victims were not just the established railway enthusiast tour operators (all but a handful of which had already been squeezed out) but organisations such as the women's institutes and working men's clubs, whose annual train trips had been a tradition. Now they were told 'Sorry – no spare vehicles'. The only beneficiaries of the stock withdrawals were Britain's independent steam lines, who eagerly snapped up ready-to-run coaches from around £1,000 a time.

Maunsell N15 4-6-0 No 777 Sir Lamiel *pounds up to Harbury tunnel with the up Shakespeare Limited for Marylebone in July 1986. This is one of BR's regular steam-hauled Sunday dining trains.*

At an early stage in the proceedings, SLOA recognised that, with the phasing out of Mk 1 stock, main-line steam operation (successfully revived in 1971) was in jeopardy. Steam's incompatibility with modern, air-braked, electrically heated Mk 2 and Mk 3 stock, was absolute. Thoughts of acquiring a complete rake of steam-compatible Mk 1s from BR were aired for the first time in 1977. The announcement in April 1981 that SLOA had bought a rake of eight Pullman cars, mounted on 100mph Commonwealth bogies and fitted with dual steam/electric heating, seemed to be the answer to a prayer. They came complete with David Ward's recommendation, and an assurance that the price, though never publicly disclosed, was 'generous'. The set was to be maintained by BR at Carlisle Upperby depot under contract. It had a total seating capacity of 378. In BR's blue-and-grey standard coach livery, later to be repainted in classic Pullman umber and cream, the Pullmans made their SLOA debut behind 'Back Five' No 5407 on the Carlisle-Hellifield *Cumbrian Mountain Pullman* on 2 May 1981. Yet even before that special had run, SLOA secretary Bernard Staite was announcing that the Pullmans would form the basis of a new series of special charter trains, operating during the summer months with diesel and electric haulage, under the title Pullman Scenic Land Cruises. This was the first time the phrase Scenic Land Cruise had been used by a train operator – but it certainly was not the last. If the move up-market started anywhere, it was on Saturday 4 July 1981, when SLOA ran the first PSLC over the Settle & Carlisle and down the Appleby–Warcop branch, for what now seems a very modest fare of £15 first class, £12

SLOA special The West Highlander is caught near Crianlarich on 1 June 1985. Motive power for this King's Cross to Mallaig train is provided by Nos 37081 Loch Long *and 37111* Loch Eil Outward Bound *over the West Highland section. The train is now run by BR and originates from St Pancras.*

second class from London (Euston), together with a tray meal at £2!

By 1983 the SLOA Pullman Scenic Land Cruise had become a series of one- and two-day charter trains with overnight hotel accommodation, embracing a variety of destinations – but most significantly, the Scottish rail routes to Mallaig, Oban, Inverness and Kyle of Lochalsh. Despite what was then described as the worst financial recession for fifty years, the Mallaig train sold out in just nine days, there being no shortage of takers for seats which by now were creeping up towards the £40 mark, and beyond the pockets of the traditional excursion-train traveller.

As a special train, the Land Cruise was a cut above its immediate predecessors, and in the ensuing years its profile and format have been further refined into a series of repeat itinerary three-day tours which, although still plying the scenic Scottish routes, now do so as part of InterCity's charter operation utilising specially refurbished first-class stock and Mk 3 sleepers in lieu of the Pullmans.

But in terms of luxury, elegance and sophistication, the Land Cruise was (and is) poles apart from the *Venice Simplon Orient Express* unleashed on an unsuspecting world in May 1982. Back came all the romance of train travel that had not been seen for fifty years. Reviving the classical grandeur of the railway carriage of Edwardian days, with all its silver-plated, lace-tableclothed dining-car finery and mahogany-panelled parlour-car ambience, on the long-established route from London to Paris and Venice, the *Orient Express* was the brainchild of James Sherwood, head of the Sea Containers Group.

Sherwood's idea was to start his all-Pullman train from London's Victoria station, and run to Folkestone where passengers would disembark, make the cross-Channel sailing to Boulogne, and continue their journey by rail to Venice via Paris and Milan. That the classical wooden-bodied Pullman cars of earlier days had long since been split up and sold or scrapped was no deterrent. Where others would have dismissed the idea as impractical, Sherwood set about locating those vehicles which had survived intact. Nine Pullmans were restored to their former splendour (but with modern air braking) at Carnforth in a remarkable £3 million project. Late in 1989 a tenth Pullman was undergoing 'the treatment' at an expected cost of £400,000. Across the Channel, Sherwood had indulged in a similar restoration exercise with a variety of former Wagons-Lits coaches, arranging the professional refurbishment of the sleeping cars, diners, day cars and staff vehicles by the Wagon-Lits shops at Ostende, and the Bremer Waggonbau company at Bremen.

In eight years of operation, the VSOE charter train has not strayed far from its original concept. The departures from London on Thursdays and Sundays between the end of February and mid-November (the return leg departs Venice on Wednesdays and Saturdays) have become well established in the BR timetable. A natural target for tourists – Americans and Japanese are especially evident during the high season – the popularity of the VSOE has been spread by tourism agencies, word of mouth, and occasional advertising in the up-market Sunday colour supplements – a clear indication of where VSOE Ltd sees its main market. In 1989 passengers undertaking the full journey from London to Venice paid a one-way fare of £745 each for a double cabin with all meals included but drinks extra. Combined train and air options have proved popular. Anyone minded just to sample VSOE Pullman luxury on 'the British bit' – and many do – could travel Victoria–Folkestone return, with champagne, lunch, a half-bottle of wine and afternoon cream tea thrown in, for £125.

Increased usage of the VSOE Pullman train for repeat itinerary charter work on days when it is not required for the Folkestone run, has given prospective passengers some further options. In 1989 a luncheon-train round trip of the Kent coast from Victoria via Canterbury and Ashford at £110, alternated on Fridays with a 'day out to Salisbury' charter special for the cathedral. Similarly, VSOE deployed the Pullmans on Wednesdays, their destination alternating between Bristol/Bath and Goodwood House/Arundel Castle. Also in demand for private and company charter hire such as conference and product launches, the one-time roadside diner and spring company board room accumulated some 400,000 miles in the eight years of operation since their 'second coming' in 1982.

Yet the title of 'the world's most luxurious train' was snatched away in 1985 by a still more exclusive charter operation introduced to British metals by a company which owned none of its own locomotives or coaching stock. The six-day *Royal Scotsman* promoted by the L & R Leisure Group under the trading name The Great Scottish & Western Railway Company, was either a remarkable piece of opportunism, or a very shrewd example of business judgement. Or both. The nine-coach train carrying just twenty-eight passengers each paying around £2,600 a time, was billed as 'the highest point yet reached in luxury train travel', its on-train cuisine described as 'simply the best on any train anywhere in the world'.

Originating at Edinburgh Waverley the *Royal Scotsman* set out to make stately progress through the mountains and glens of the Scottish Highlands, with a package of sightseeing visits to ancient castles and gardens, country houses and distilleries in store for its well-heeled patrons. Despite its somewhat unmatched look, the stock formation included some pearls of the Victorian railway era, such as an 1891 ex-LNWR dining saloon, and a Caledonian observation car originally built in 1892, together with a varnished teak Great Northern family saloon of 1912. Sleeping cars with en-suite bathroom, shower and toilet were barely recognisable as the BR Mk 1 vehicles from which they had been skilfully converted. This is truly a 'cruise train' with all facilities on board as on a luxury liner.

The whole train, attired in the plum-and-spilt-milk livery of the LNWR and Caledonian Railways, had been assembled together by Rick Edmondson, then chairman of Rotherham diesel locomotive manufacturers Thomas Hill, and leased to the Great Scottish & Western Railway Company, under a five-year agreement. One of the principal highlights of the *Royal Scotsman* was steam haulage over the superbly scenic forty-one-mile section between Fort

William and Mallaig – the romantic 'Road to the Isles' – using one of the two locomotives stabled at Fort William for BR's own summer excursion trains; and from 1986 over the independent Strathspey Railway's five-mile line between Aviemore and Boat of Garten as well.

The durability of the *Royal Scotsman* over five long seasons of operation, with the top tour price now only a short step away from £3,000 was proven by 1989, but even as this book was being prepared for press, there were changes in the wind which may prove to be a sterner test of the depth of the elitist train-tour market. Both the Great Scottish & Western Railway Co and the coaching stock owner were proposing to operate a 'top people's train' independently of each other in 1990!

Taking British Rail itself into the VIP train market was an altogether different matter. There was no easy route. In 1984, when the InterCity Charter Unit was first set up, it had at its disposal some twenty sets of Mk 1 stock – principally second-class tourist open vehicles – but nothing which

No 47487 hauls a King's Cross to Chester-le-Street charter near Stonebridge, Durham on 27 June 1985. The stock is mostly refurbished InterCity Mk1 vehicles.

could credibly be described as suitable for the VIP trains it was seeking to introduce. Progressively reducing the twenty Mk 1 sets by half, and acquiring from regular service stock a fleet of Mk 1 first open coaches, Ward put in hand a programme of vehicle refurbishment involving re-upholstering, re-carpeting and curtain replacement and the fitting of individual table lamps, with the aim of restoring a level of respectability to coaches which had seen better days. During the second half of the eighties, InterCity could at last boast five complete ten-coach VIP train sets all based and serviced at London's Bounds Green depot. They comprised four Mk 1 FO sets, each made up of seven FO saloons, two kitchen cars and a BFK brake vehicle, plus the former *Manchester Pullman* set of seven parlour cars, two parlour

Traditional roast dinner is served in one of InterCity's refurbished Mk1 open coaches. Note the table lamps.

kitchen cars and a parlour brake. All were outshopped in standard InterCity 'raspberry ripple' coach livery but distinguished from ordinary service stock by having white-painted roofs.

For up-market small-party charter hire, InterCity also procured the former London Midland Region general manager's saloon No 6320 – something of a hybrid, comprising a special body on a Mk 1 underframe and B4 bogies, which had been converted for dual braking and electric train heating. In addition, there is a single HST Mk 3 saloon, which, since special refitting to include a lounge and dining area, has seen use by both the Queen and the Prime Minister. The Charter Unit's second-class sets, or more correctly standard class sets as BR now prefers to describe them, also underwent refurbishment during the tail end of the 1980s with twenty-four of the Mk 1 TSOs being smartened up and fitted for air braking during 1988, and a further twelve earmarked for the same treatment during the early part of 1990.

Because BR is reluctant to talk about profits, it is difficult to gauge accurately how successful InterCity's forage into the top end of the charter-train market has been, or how much the total earnings from charter traffic contribute to the sector's overall profitability. But there is little doubt that charter-train profit can be read in seven-figure sums rather than six and that as a business venture, InterCity has not done badly at all. Nevertheless InterCity cheerfully reveals that the VIP/first-class/full-dining trains contribute by far the largest share of the special-trains earnings – 50 per cent – compared with the 23 per cent from private charters, 18 per cent by standard-class charters, and 5 per cent by the steam market. Exhibition-train revenue makes up the final 4 per cent.

The aces in the pack are undoubtedly high quality business charters and the three-day Scenic Land Cruise trains. The latter became InterCity property in 1986, following a long and complicated sequence of events which began near the end of 1983 with the enforced withdrawal of the SLOA Pullman set, following the discovery that the potentially dangerous blue asbestos coach body insulation had become exposed. Unable to meet the huge cost of the highly specialised asbestos de-contamination work then demanded of the entire Pullman set, SLOA agreed to sell the Pullmans to industrialist Sir William McAlpine (better known to railway enthusiasts as the owner of *Flying Scotsman*) and to hire them back for steam-charter use once the asbestos stripping work was complete. Under McAlpine's 'Pullman Rail' banner, the Pullmans returned to railtour duties in September 1984 – but by now Pullman Rail, with former SLOA secretary Bernard Staite as managing director, had also acquired from BR a second full rake of coaches – Mk 1 first opens, ostensibly for steam railtour work. The Pullmans, it was announced, would be kept more or less exclusively for Pullman Rail's newly created non-steam-charter haul business. After four months back in traffic however, the discovery of further traces of blue asbestos on parts of the Pullman underframes, caused the set to be impounded again . . . at which point InterCity took the initiative to run its own refurbished VIP stock on the Scenic Land Cruise trains, albeit with Pullman Rail contracted to continue booking the trains. In January 1988, the name Pullman Rail was dropped by McAlpine, in favour of 'Flying Scotsman Services'.

As the 1980s were drawing to their close, *The West Highlander* – not to be confused with the BR-promoted summer steam service of the same name running between Fort William and Mallaig – emerged as the Charter Unit's most successful train, achieving an average load factor of 87 per cent. With 156 passengers representing a full trainload, and high-season tickets (end of May – end of July) selling at £320, one does not have to be a brilliant mathematician to get a grasp of the kind of revenue being earned.

The inclusion in the Land Cruise trainset of seven first-class sleeping cars, coupled to InterCity's insistence that every passenger should have a window seat, stretched the *West Highlander* formation to sixteen vehicles – too long for the platforms at King's Cross which could cope with only fourteen – so by default the Friday evening departure was written down to St Pancras, picking up at St Albans and Derby. By way of example, the highlights of the 1989 train itinerary looked something like this:

Friday: Depart St Pancras. Dinner served on train. Overnight berth at Stirling.

Saturday: Depart Stirling for Oban. Passenger ferry to Craignure on the Isle of Mull for a tour not only of Mull but a visit to Iona. Overnight hotel at Fort William.

Sunday: Depart Fort William for Mallaig, with a cruise on Loch Nevis followed by a stop for Glenfinnan Monument visit. Depart Fort William for overnight berth at Stirling.

Monday: Depart Stirling for Edinburgh. Three-hour visit for shopping. Lunch served on train to include Haggis and Neeps, Cock-a-Leekie soup, Noisettes of Lamb or Poached Scotch Salmon, Pineapple Pavlova. Arrive St Pancras.

A far cry from the £2 tray meal handed out on the first of the Scenic Land Cruise trains eight years earlier, in a decade of special-train running where sophistication got its chance – and left behind many ordinary folk for whom the railway 'excursion' is now but a fading memory.

6
NETWORK SOUTHEAST

NOWHERE did the 1980s have a greater impact than on the services which at sectorisation became Network SouthEast (NSE). At the decade's start everything was gloom and doom, cutbacks the order of the day since in 1979 the number of commuters going into London dropped for the tenth successive year. By 1989 the problems were of growth and too buoyant demand stretching the resources though those had been considerably augmented. Not merely was the transformation great in itself but, of course, on the largest commuter network under single ownership in the world – equating to the complete Dutch or Belgian railways, carrying two million passengers daily and accounting for 41 per cent of all commuters into central London. When reading this chapter, remember that not merely is NSE the largest of BR's

Refurbished 4-Cep unit No 1585 in London and South East Express two-tone brown (jaffa cake) livery comes under the impressive signal-box at Canterbury West working as the 12.03 Margate to Charing Cross via Ashford on 23 September 1986.

businesses but in 1989 ranked as the 106th largest business of every kind in Britain.

Briefly to record the miserable 1970s, London's rail commuters faced fare increases of 40 per cent between June 1974 and May 1975. BR could not avoid passing its dramatically increased costs following the oil crisis on to its customers, especially London commuters, and as they reduced in number (demand falling at 1 per cent a year) services, stock and facilities were reduced to 'match demand', inevitably causing poor morale. Even the ever-ebullient Sir Peter Parker saw parts of the commuter system 'rattling into decline', and nobody was surprised when in 1979 the government referred the services to the Monopolies & Mergers Commission. The Commission's report was perhaps the turning point, for while it paid respect to the management it found 'to be totally dedicated to the railway with a high degree of pride in the service which came before financial reward in importance', it made thought-provoking recommendations about management style and the need to set clearer financial objectives. In particular BR were advised to create a new senior post at headquarters with special responsibility for London and the South East.

How did the transformation come about? Like Caesar's Gaul, it can be described in three parts: continuing decline 1980–2; the London & South Eastern phase under David Kirby 1982–5; and the reign of Chris Green and the birth of Network SouthEast commencing with his appointment on 6 January 1986. Just how great the change has been is perhaps best illustrated

The 11.20 'Bedpan' service from St Pancras to Bedford departs the London terminus on 26 September 1986 formed of Class 317/0 emu No 317315.

by reference to the number of daily commuters into London. The decline was finally arrested in 1984; in the next four years the losses of the previous fourteen were made good! Let us look at it year by year.

1980, the year of Continuing Decline. BR could claim that even before the Monopoly Commission report's comments on the need for a new rolling-stock policy it was moving towards the development of stock for use on all regions, having introduced Class 313 25kV AC/750V DC (dual voltage) inner-suburban stock in 1976 for the Great Northern electrification scheme followed in 1978 by Class 507 750V DC third-rail stock for Merseyrail (Midland Region); and Class 314 25kV AC stock in Scotland. From 7 January 1980, Class 508 750V DC stock commenced all-day operation on the south-western division of Southern Region and later in the year Class 315 units were introduced on Great Eastern line services from Liverpool Street. Albeit with differing electrical systems, these units were of similar external appearance and brought to the Southern Region for the first time (other than on the Waterloo & City line and the experimental PEP unit) sliding-door stock which might ultimately be suitable for one-person operation.

Elsewhere on Southern Region (where main-line passengers could see no prospect of new stock) 1980 saw the introduction of the first refurbished 4-CEP (Class 411) unit No 411506. These main-line electric multiple units had been built between 1959 and 1963 for the Kent Coast electrification with a design life of approximately twenty-five years. To all intents and purposes, the body shells of the old units were rebuilt above the solebar at Swindon Works and new (and considered by many less comfortable) seats with removable cushion covers, fluorescent lighting, double-glazed windows and a public address system were installed to extend their working lives into the twenty-first century! With their infamous riding qualities, the units compared ill with the air-conditioned delights of Mark 3 and HST stock being introduced on other regions.

But despite the still-falling demand, 1980 was not all gloom and doom. It saw the signing of a contract worth £15.5million with Westinghouse Brake & Signal Company for the construction of a new power signalbox at Three Bridges as part of a £45million scheme for resignalling the whole of the Brighton main line. The new box was to replace thirty-three existing signalboxes and to control the line between Norwood Junction and Brighton, including Gatwick Airport which, from May 1980, was to be the terminus of a new semi-fast cross-country service from Reading (via Guildford and Redhill).

11 June saw the reopening of a station closed thirty-five years previously and the opening of the first new inner-London station for very many years: Hackney Central and Hackney Wick on the 'Cross Town Link Line' between North Woolwich and Camden Road, a promise of greater things to come.

1981. Quiet Consolidation. Only one station was reopened, Kentish Town West on the North London line, on 5 October by Ken Livingstone, leader of the GLC which had entirely funded the £400,000 rebuilding costs. But on the Southern Region, ⅜ mile Laverstock loop (last used in 1859) was reinstated at Salisbury linking the Basingstoke and Romsey lines as part of the £2million Salisbury resignalling scheme. This scheme was relatively modest in comparison with many others such as the £7million scheme, for which contracts were this year placed to resignal fifty-six route miles from Cambridge to Royston, Bishop's Stortford, Fulbourne (on the line to Newmarket) and to a point just south of Ely.

But even more important for travellers in East Anglia was the announcement, just before Christmas, of the approval of part of the Anglian electrification scheme (to Norwich and Harwich).

On 12 January the Midland electrification between Luton and Bedford went live in preparation for driver-only training.

1982. The Year of Dispute and Sectorisation. That training (and the service that should have started with the Class 317 units at the beginning of the 1982 timetable) was stopped by an industrial dispute about bonus payments for driver-only operation. It became entwined with the separate dispute with ASLEF over flexible rostering, which the board had announced would be introduced from July with or without agreement. ASLEF called out its members on a strike, described by Sir Peter Parker as 'deplorable and shameful', from 3 July. With government imposing pressure by withdrawing its PSO grant of £15.5million per week, and a mixed response from ASLEF members that enabled the board to run approximately 1,500 passenger trains and 150 freight trains each weekday, a peace formula was worked out and normal services were resumed on 19 July. The disruption contributed to the still-declining commuter business. But some positive things happened in 1982 like the opening of Milton Keynes Central at a cost of £4.5million; Watton-at-Stone between Stevenage and Hertford North; and of Watford Stadium on the Watford Junction–Croxley Green branch on 4 December. And it was in 1982 that David Kirby was appointed director of the new London & South East sector. But he remained general manager of the Southern Region, almost as it were being his own superior. He was (in retrospect) surprisingly luke warm about the potential of cross-London links – 'show me the market' – although he was no doubt pleased to accept in this first year in office an offer from the GLC to fund the third-rail electrification over 8½ miles between Dalston and North Woolwich.

1983. Turning the Corner. The economy was improving, and evidence of increased confidence within L&SE can be found in 1983 in the eventual introduction of electric one-person-operated trains between Moorgate, St Pancras and Bedford; the opening of no less than four new stations; and government approval for the long awaited electrification of the Tonbridge–Hastings line. After its well publicised trials and tribulations, limited electric working from St Pancras commenced on 28 March and the electric service was officially inaugurated by the Secretary of State, Tom King, on 15 July. A full service was introduced in the following year after various problems with

the new units had been resolved. New stations opened during 1983 included Pinhoe (Devon) on the very edge of the L&SE boundary, Templecombe, and Dalston Kingsland on the Camden Road–North Woolwich Cross Town Link line. The latter, built on the site of a station closed as long ago as 1865, was wholly funded by the GLC and the Department of Environment's urban programme grant.

There were also closures such as the short section of electrified line between Elmers End and Sanderstead (near Croydon), Coulsdon North to enable Brighton line resignalling works to proceed, and Broad Street as a pre-requisite of the redevelopment of Liverpool Street.

Evidence that David Kirby was keen to show that L&SE was no longer a region-based organisation is to be found in the launch of Awayday, entitling an adult, if accompanied by at least one child, to purchase up to four additional tickets for adults or children at a flat fare of £1 each for use anywhere within the sector area.

1984. Take-off and Gatwick Express. For the first time in fourteen years the peak-hour commuter figures show growth (a modest half per cent) but an

No 50029 Renown approaches Exeter Central station with the 09.15 Waterloo to Exeter St David's on 17 August 1989. The whole train is in NSE colours and includes Mk2A and B vehicles.

83

interview with David Kirby indicated that L&SE had no inkling of what was to come. Indeed, David Kirby stressed how the L&SE call on the PSO grant would be limited by a continued reduction in fleet size (from 7,465 vehicles to 7,050 vehicles within two years) and by running fewer and shorter trains to adapt to 'reduced demand'. The only opportunity for a large increase in revenue was thought to lie in the *Gatwick Express* non-stop service introduced in May, featuring air-conditioned stock on the half-hour journey from Victoria to Gatwick every fifteen minutes (and powered on a push-pull basis by Class 73 electro-diesels). One of the locomotives (No 73123) was named *Gatwick Express* and turned out in a new livery to match the refurbished Mark 2 stock. (The successful service was transferred to InterCity in 1985.)

In July the Southern's south-east, central and south-west divisions were abolished, new passenger business manager posts created and a reduced number of area manager posts (but each with increased responsibility) set up. This was part of a new drive, following criticism in the Serpell Report that the railway was too 'production led' to become more businesslike. The joint BR/LRT Capitalcard for the following year was announced, along with plans to electrify from Bishop's Stortford to Cambridge, on the East Coast main line to Huntingdon, and between Romford and Upminster.

1985. To Thameslink and Beyond. In the light of its subsequent success, the most important event was the authorisation of a £54million scheme to link

A unique view of Holborn Viaduct photographed from a well placed office window on 18 August 1989. Class 319 No 319041 forms the 15.56 Luton–Brighton 'Thameslink' service emerging from Snow Hill tunnel while above Class 413/2 4-CAPS Nos 3206 (heading the 16.54 to Kent House) and 3207 (leading the 16.47 to Canterbury East) await their respective departure times.

the Midland and Southern electrified systems by reinstating the half-mile-long disused tunnel between Farringdon and Blackfriars. Reopening of the tunnel, which had last seen regular passenger services in 1916 and goods traffic in 1969, had been considered in the London Rail Study in 1974 but rejected because the cost (including a new interchange station at West Hampstead) had been estimated at £30million. A more realistic and simple proposal was investigated by the GLC who concluded that it might be possible to reopen the link for as little as £1million. The £54million package now authorised included the cost of forty six four-car dual-voltage electric units, the introduction of which would enable a greater number of existing units to be withdrawn because of more efficient use. Within months it became obvious that increased demand on the Midland electrified lines (at last free from industrial problems and stock defects) would make additional units necessary. Fourteen additional units were authorised in May 1986, by which time traffic on the Midland electrified lines had increased by 50 per cent since electrification.

Electrification was announced over the eighteen-mile stretch between Sanderstead and East Grinstead (but excluding the Uckfield branch). This scheme was justified by the withdrawal of asbestos-bearing diesel multiple units and by the more efficient use of the existing EMU fleet; the withdrawal of asbestos-bearing stock was also one of the grounds for the Bournemouth–Weymouth electrification scheme submitted during the year.

From 13 May electric operation actually commenced between Dalston and North Woolwich, and a new £440,000 station jointly funded by the GLC and the Department of the Environment opened at Homerton (between Hackney Wick and Hackney Central) on the site of a station closed in 1944. In contrast, 5 July saw the end of the already very limited service between Stratford and Tottenham Hale via Lea Bridge, a line which may now return to passenger use following electrification at 25kV in 1989.

The image of LSE was enhanced by David Kirby's decision to introduce a new livery unique to LSE. It was revealed when 'Essex Express' unit No 309605 was handed over on completion of refurbishment at Wolverton Works under a £17.5million contract in March. The refurbished unit enjoyed a 26 per cent increase in seating capacity and was finished in a two-tone brown livery embellished with an orange band at waist level. This 'Jaffa cake' scheme was soon also to be adopted for main-line Class 411 stock by the south-east sub-sector of Southern Region.

1986. Network SouthEast. 1986 saw the arrival of Chris Green as Sector director (on 6 January) and its dramatic re-launch six months later as Network SouthEast. There was suitable razzamatazz at Waterloo on 10 June when the blue/white/red/grey livery was shown to the press on two Class 455 units and a Class 50 *Howe* hauling a short rake of Mark 2 coaches.

L&SE went out with a bang rather than a whimper. 12 May was marked by the introduction of no less than four new electric services; on the Eastern Region branch lines between Wickford and Southminster and between

Romford and Upminster; on the Great Eastern main line between Manning-tree and Harwich; and (at last) over the thirty-two miles between Tonbridge and Hastings. The Hastings £20m scheme was celebrated by a successful 'Gala Day' on 27 April when unlimited travel over the line for only £1 was available and more formally on 6 May when the Queen Mother (Lord Warden of the Cinque Ports) travelled over the line in the Royal Train. In preparation for electrification, sufficient Class 411 units had been repainted in 'Jaffa cake' livery and branded the '1066 Electrics' to give added impact.

Also on 12 May, and with financial assistance from Berkshire County Council and the developer of an adjoining industrial estate, a new station opened at Winnersh Triangle on the Southern Region line on the outskirts of Reading. Another new station opened on 29 September at Welham Green (between Hatfield and Brookmans Park).

During David Kirby's period as head of L&SE, the sector's call on the public service obligation grant had fallen by 36 per cent during three years, and Chris Green's task was to reduce (if not ultimately obviate the need for) the grant. NSE's name, and livery, was chosen to give a new character and significance to the rail system in the south east, and to emphasise its unity as a system, no longer a series of independent lines owning loyalty not to London as a whole but to long-abolished independent railway companies. He aimed to increase off-peak travel in particular by enhancing the quality of travel and station environment by 'Operation Pride', a name coined to launch the quality improvement drive, and by new and imaginative marketing exercises, one of the first of which was a 'Network Day' on 21 June when over 200,000 people took advantage of the special £3 ticket enabling them to travel all day anywhere. So successful was the exercise, in both revenue and public relation terms, that a further 'Network Day' was held on 13 September. The same 10 June also saw the launch of the one-day Capitalcard giving (after the morning peak) unlimited travel on BR, London Underground, London Buses and (in due course) Docklands Light Railway. Within twelve months it had exceeded expectations and become a £40million growth product. Further growth in leisure travel (which represents 29 per cent of NSE income) was planned to follow the introduction of the 'Network Card' on 29 September providing one-third discounts on off-peak travel.

Chris Green announced that NSE had a commitment to quality improve-ments on all fronts, but with full-blooded business direction aimed at maximising the high profile of the sector, to which his famous red lamp posts gave an immediate impact. Longer term financial and quality improvements were to follow major station redevelopment schemes, including profit-producing office and retail elements, of which the redevelopment of Liverpool Street and for which new plans were announced in 1986 is a good example. The redevelopment of Liverpool Street involved the closure of the much decayed ex-North London Railway terminus at Broad Street, and the diversion from 30 June of the remaining North London Line services to the City via the newly constructed Graham Road curve into Liverpool Street using dual-voltage Class 313 units.

In retrospect the most important event of 1986 may have been the conception of the new Networker train, filling a vital gap price and quality wise, at long last making it possible for NSE to plan systematic replacement of old EMUs.

1987. The Year of Electrification. On 19 January electric trains began operation between Bishop's Stortford and Cambridge, and within three months authority was received to electrify the nearby ten-mile gap from Royston to Shepreth Branch Junction (near Cambridge), the anticipated £2.5million costs being justified by savings in the use of rolling stock and lower maintenance costs. Next month, full electric services commenced between Cambridge and Liverpool Street; between Norwich and Liverpool Street (partly sponsored by InterCity) and between Peterborough and King's Cross. To celebrate its joining the electric network, Cambridge was visited on 23 March by the Minister of Transport (David Mitchell) on a record-breaking (48 minute) trip from Liverpool Street.

The May timetable also saw the reintroduction of a limited and experimental passenger service between Oxford and Bicester Town (previously Bicester London Road before closure in January 1968), sponsored by Oxford City and County Councils, Cherwell District and Bicester Town Councils as a possible partial solution to traffic congestion in Oxford. Subsequently, the Bicester service, although still indicated as experimental in the public timetable, has been enhanced and an intermediate station opened at Islip. A month earlier, another experimental service reopened between Kettering and

The 11.02 Dartford–Charing Cross with 4-EPB No 5335 leading passes the new Eltham station under construction on 17 August 1984. This station replaced Eltham Well Hall and Eltham Park.

Corby with as many as seventeen trains daily. On the former GWR line to Bicester North a new station opened in October at Haddenham & Thame Parkway – the 150th new station opened by BR since the Beeching cuts of the 1960s. A new station at Lake (near Shanklin) on the Isle of Wight showed NSE's commitment to retaining the railway on the island.

More passengers have of course benefitted from the electrification of the Oxted and East Grinstead lines, although railway euphoria was possibly dampened by the Minister of Transport who on 30 September took the opportunity of rejecting further recommendations by the Monopoly Commission that increased investment was necessary to provide a satisfactory quality of service on NSE. The East Grinstead scheme had only been authorised because of the need to replace asbestos-infected elderly diesel multiple units and by demonstrating that no new rolling stock would be required.

New stock was of course required for the proposed Thameslink service, and Chris Green formally accepted the first Class 319 dual-voltage unit at BREL York on 2 September. Also welcome was the Royal Assent to the Bill authorising the construction of spurs from the Liverpool Street–Cambridge line to serve Stansted Airport on which work is now substantially advanced.

Class 321 emu No 321307 takes the Cambridge line through the Bethnal Green station platforms on 10 January 1989 forming the 13.05 Liverpool Street– Cambridge train while, on the right, the 11.37 Harwich Town–Liverpool Street service is formed of Class 312/1 emus Nos 312793/784.

1988. Thameslink and Wessex Electrics. The pace quickened, this year seeing the long-awaited introduction of the Thameslink service, the extension of electrification from Bournemouth to Weymouth and the delivery (albeit late) of Class 442 'Wessex Electrics' units to give air-conditioned comfort to NSE passengers. But 1988 ended with the disaster at Clapham discussed in the signalling chapter.

Given its success after only eighteen months, and the current plans to extend the Thameslink network, it now seems hard to believe that passengers have enjoyed the ability to cross London by regular electric BR services for

such a short time. Success has been despite the somewhat confusing route plan initially imposed on the service south of the Thames by the necessity of incorporating the new service into an existing timetable without increasing mileage. Thameslink was formally inaugurated by HRH The Princess Royal on 25 April, when she combined its formal launch with that of Save the Children Week and travelled with a number of children on unit 319036 to Crystal Palace. The everyday Thameslink service commenced on 16 May.

The initial order for sixty Class 319 units was soon increased to eighty-six. Later in 1988 these units began to be joined north of the Thames by similar (but AC current only) units of Class 321 for use on Cambridge and Northampton services for which sixty-eight units were authorised, together with a further five similar Class 322 units for the Stansted Airport link.

The Class 321 units (of which the first was delivered in September 1988), were an immediate success, but the same cannot be said of the Class 442 'Wessex Electrics' of which twenty-four five-car units should have been delivered in time for the May 1988 timetable. In fact, only four units were available in May. Southern Region general manager Gordon Pettitt took a calculated gamble when he authorised a charity high-speed run to Weymouth on 14 April, when the special train completed the 142½ mile trip to Weymouth in seconds within two hours with a maximum speed of 109mph.

On the London Midland Region, electric trains of Class 313 commenced running, a year earlier than anticipated, between Watford Junction and St Albans Abbey on 11 July, on which line a further new station – How Wood – opened later in the year. Class 313 units are also used on the suburban service between Euston and Watford Junction, to which service fell the honour of being the first line to be given a NSE total route refurbishment programme and branded 'Harlequin'. The programme included station and train refurbishment, new train information systems and full resignalling. Experience on this line, as earlier on the Midland Suburban line and subsequently on the North London, has demonstrated the marketing advantages and associated traffic growth that follow such schemes. It may well have contributed to the 1989 decision to introduce a policy of 'Power to the Routes' for the current decade. Fifteen separate routes have been made the responsibility of managers whose chief aim is to satisfy their customers. In the words of Chris Green: 'Every problem will at last have an owner.'

The lot of the Great Northern manager was eased in November by the reopening of an additional suburban platform (No 11) at King's Cross. The Minister of Transport initiated electrification of twenty-eight route miles in Hampshire between Portsmouth and Southampton and Eastleigh, to be finished in 1990. To the east, management within NSE was assisted by the creation on 29 April of a new Anglia Region covering lines serving Liverpool Street and Fenchurch Street stations.

1989. Looking to the Future. Hot on the Clapham accident, five passengers were killed in a collision at Purley (south of Croydon), again involving two Southern Region electric multiple units.

Save for the opening of a further station, at Islip on the Oxford–Bicester Town line, it was a year of consolidation and planning. Class 321 units continued to be delivered at the rate of two a week, and on the Isle of Wight 'new' 1938-built former London Underground trains began to be introduced to replace coaches dating from 1923. Authority was obtained for the modernisation of the Chiltern line between Marylebone and Banbury via Bicester including resignalling and the provision of seventy-seven Class 165 Networker coaches, and in August the then new Minister of Transport, Cecil Parkinson, authorised the first hundred Networker four-car trains for the North Kent lines.

The decade could hardly have ended on a more optimistic note. While it has to be obvious that current success has been built on foundations that were perhaps sounder than people generally thought ten years ago, the combination of a livelier economy and greater commercial drive (leading above all to more commonsense, usually more local management) has produced results far above the most rosy forecasts. The pride taken not only by many staff but passengers in their more clearly identified 'Lines' is paying handsome dividends. But four main factors are singled out by Chris Green for the currently greatly improved outlook: the record investment currently being made, at the end of 1989 amounting to an astonishing million pounds a day; the success of the Networker train whose carriages in 1989 were being delivered at the rate of one a day; the enormous level of London station development both enhancing the environment (who at the start of the 1980s would have thought of treating a terminus as a shopping precinct?) and producing revenue on the grand scale; and the steady introduction of Integrated Electronic Control Centres (discussed in detail in the signalling chapter). As mentioned at the start of this chapter, forecasts made at the end of the 1970s now seem horribly pessimistic. It is hard to envisage the total 1990s story, but the decade starts with greater confidence in the railways serving London and the South East than, perhaps since Victorian times.

Looking to the future! Breaking the banner at Ryde Pier Head to inaugurate the first run of the Eastleigh-refurbished ex-LT 1938 stock from Ryde Pier Head to Brading on 13 July 1989, Class 483 unit No 001 looks particularly smart in a neater version of NSE livery.

7
PROVINCIAL

WHO would have thought, back in 1980, that we would now be reading in the popular railway magazines a number of reports that British Rail's Provincial sector possesses some routes which are promising to become profitable? Who indeed could have forecast that the Provincial sector would be announcing such an improvement in their financial situation resulting from rapid but targeted investment in new trains, with the prime objective of cost reduction?

Certainly, only eight years ago, when the other sectors were given clearly defined briefs, the lumping of unprofitable passenger services into a somewhat negatively titled 'Other Provincial Services' produced a kind of dustbin sector.

Provincial inherited a very wide range of types of route, train make-up, and service level. It had very few jewels in its crown. Possibly the Edinburgh–Glasgow push-pull trains represented the sector's highest quality product, being formed of Mark 3 stock and powered by smart and newly overhauled Class 47/7 locomotives. Other internal Scottish Region expresses to Aberdeen and Inverness also became part of the Provincial empire, even though their carriages were still branded 'InterCity' for many years after sectorisation. There was also the Liverpool–Newcastle service, which in other countries would have been given 'InterCity' status, and which shared tracks north of Leeds with InterCity trains, but which ran here with older stock, Mark 1 or early Mark 2, hauled by the heavy and increasingly unreliable 1Co-Co1 locomotives of Classes 40 or 46.

If those trains represented the top quality of Provincial's empire, there was much less to be excited about elsewhere. Outside the large conurbations, which were the province of the locally financed Passenger Transport Executives, Provincial inherited a disparate collection of routes linking various centres or branching to less populous places. Many routes could not be said to form a coherent network, other than as InterCity connections to whom they did not now belong, and a few (surprisingly few) were in the mould of the traditional country branch line. Most of the secondary routes that survive are relatively long, run through sparsely populated land, and have no hope of making money. In this category one can group the West Highland and Kyle lines, the Central Wales, the Cambrian and Cumbrian coast, and possibly the Suffolk coast line.

The rest are mainly either inter-urban routes like Portsmouth-Bristol, quite busy branch lines like the Cornish branches or the South Wales branches; or

The 1980s saw the extensive refurbishment of the ageing Class 31 fleet and a need for more eth fitted Class 31/4s. Here two examples are seen at Gilberdyke. No 31466 halts at the platform with the 13.39 Lancaster to Hull service while No 31439 passes non-stop with the 15.50 Hull to Lancaster on 16 August 1985. This section of line is now double track and the station platforms have been altered to serve the middle roads on this picture. During the late 1980s the line to Doncaster was severed when the swing-bridge over the River Ouse at Goole was damaged by a Swedish freighter on 23 November 1988.

they are former main lines from which InterCity has progressively withdrawn – like the Settle & Carlisle, the former Glasgow & South Western Glasgow route, Newport–Crewe, the trans-Pennine lines and some cross-country routes crossing England from east to west. There are local stopping services which run on InterCity routes, such as the Birmingham–Rugby–Northampton electric trains, the Manchester–Blackpool trains, Edinburgh–Dunbar locals and stopping trains on the North Wales route.

The description of these services as 'disparate' surely applies also to the traction and rolling stock inherited by Provincial, the assets most responsible for the sector's cost base. The only modern-design vehicles, apart from the Scottish air-conditioned stock, were possibly the Class 310 electric multiple units radiating from Rugby, and even these dated from the mid 1960s. Everything else was either original or refurbished diesel multiple unit, or the popular but cost-ineffective combination of diesel locomotives and cast-off main line carriages.

For many lifetimes railway practice had been for locomotives and rolling stock to be downgraded or 'cascaded' from front line to secondary services. No one expected otherwise than to get second- or third-hand stock on a train running between Weymouth and Bristol, or between Manchester Victoria and Leeds, or from Glasgow to Stranraer.

The same happened to stations. The owning Regions had their priorities to maintain to reasonable standards the stations on main lines and which were the calling points for InterCity trains. In the 1970s money just was not available to smarten up more than a handful of Provincial stations. Those fortunate to be in the areas covered by the PTEs were another story.

Money or the lack of it is what had modelled the railwayman's thinking in the formative years of BR. From Dr Beeching onwards, managers were trained in the science of work study, in the discipline of financial restraint, and in being able to manage on less, to cut out or just delay expenditure. In a sector where the income from sales of tickets represented less than a quarter of total expenditure, there was little else one could expect. Thus as the recession of the early 1980s drew to its close 'condition of track' speed restrictions of some severity were imposed: for example stretches of 35 to 50mph between Selby and Hull on the straightest railway in Britain.

How, then, do we now celebrate Provincial's success as the 1990s begin? It is a fascinating story of a turnaround, of the value of sectorisation and of the quality of the managers who took up the challenge of 'Other Provincial Services'.

As a loss maker, Provincial received the bulk of its income from grants from the PTEs, and from the government in the form of the Public Service Obligation (PSO). Not surprisingly, the Department of Transport, and in consequence the British Railways Board, maintained a policy of aiming to reduce the PSO so as to reduce the demands on the taxpayer. Nationalised industries were first set annual cash limits under a Labour administration, but the concept was in line with Conservative Government policy to cut direct

taxation and release cash so that people (voters) had a greater choice with what to do with their money.

John Welsby was appointed as the first Director, Provincial, and he set about evaluating the sources of the sector's costs. Quite clearly, as costs were four times direct revenue, 10 per cent (for example) saving in costs had much more effect on the balance than did a potential 20 per cent increase in revenue, so energy was at first concentrated on the cost base. A significant feature was the realisation that BR's policy to refurbish and life-extend the ageing fleet of diesel multiple units involved an enormous additional expense in the sudden requirement to extract all their blue and white asbestos. (The asbestos had been built into the carriages to act as sound and heat insulation, but had of course later been found to be a health hazard.) The same work was also required in a large number of the early Mark 2 locomotive-hauled carriages, and in many long-life electric multiple units. It emerged that across the very varied fleets the cost of asbestos removal would be £25,000 per vehicle, an investment producing no financial return. The question had to be asked: could the purchase of new trains produce savings sufficient to cover the cost of servicing their capital costs as well as reducing the burden on the PSO?

In the 1970s there were only two types of potential replacement DMU being considered by BR's passenger marketing people and the engineers. The Class 210 diesel-electric design of three-car or four-car unit had actually been produced to a business specification developed in conjunction with the board's passenger commercial managers. It was intended as a high-performance set which could inherit the reliability associated with previous BR (SR) DEMUs, thus beating the older, inherently unreliable diesel-mechanical multiple units hands down. Its problem, when analysed by the new Provincial sector was its price: it would cost too much to enable a financial case to be made for the 210 breed to replace existing DMUs even taking asbestos removal into account.

The other design in the offing was the two-axle railbus which had started life as a Research Division project aimed at combining high-speed freight-vehicle technology with that of the standard Leyland road bus in order to produce a low cost diesel train. This was certainly a cheap option, and there were some short- or medium-distance routes where such a basic vehicle was considered acceptable. In particular the PTEs in West Yorkshire and Greater Manchester were interested in the railbus as a replacement for their ageing DMUs. Experience with these trains, delivered as Classes 141 (West Yorkshire) and 142 (Greater Manchester and elsewhere) was encouraging. Their promised availability and utilisation was such that one new vehicle was expected to replace two old ones, and thus considerable cost savings were

Expensive prototype. The three-car version of the Class 210 demu, set No 210002 departs from West Ealing with the 11.05 Paddington–Slough service on 22 February 1984. Note the main and relief lines ladder junction.

ensured. More units (Classes 143 and 144) were delivered for services in Tyneside and West Yorkshire.

The problems with the gearboxes of the 141s, 142s and 143s were well publicised as the 1980s drew into their second half. The supplying company could not keep up delivery of repaired gearboxes to match the rate at which they failed, and with low availability of their new fleet Provincial had to retain the DMUs it was supposed to replace for a couple or so more years. It also turned out that the 142s in Cornwall, and indeed those in Manchester to a lesser extent, suffered high wheel wear. This necessitated their removal from the West Country branches while those units working in the Northern conurbations needed their wheel treads reprofiling more frequently, causing another temporary source of low availability for there was a shortage of replacement wheels. But the new two-axle units were actually responsible for part of the upsurge in traffic on their routes and were certainly no worse than the buses with which they were successfully competing.

Meanwhile, however, it had become clear that there had to be a replacement DMU which was placed midway in size and cost between the railbuses and the 210 units. But, if underfloor engines and transmissions were to be used, they had to be in a different league of reliability and performance from the DMUs which BR had been running since the 1950s. Fortunately, some experience had been building up on the European continent, in Holland in particular, with DMUs which had very reliable and

Climbing the Pennines. Sprinter units Nos 150242 and 150230 pass the distant signal for Greenfield as they work the 10.03 Liverpool to Scarborough service on 31 August 1987.

cost-effective engines and transmissions. The Nederlands Railways 3100 and 3200 Class units employ Cummins diesel engines with Voith hydraulic transmission driving through permanently engaged final drives on the axles. This combination was tried among others on four prototype three-car DMUs on BR, two from BREL being Class 150 and two from Metro-Cammell being eventually known as Class 152. Thus was born the hardware of the BR Sprinter units, but their business environment needs discussing in depth because of the fundamental re-thinking which resulted from the need to maximise the potential of those trains.

When the first orders were placed the numbers of two-car units in the fleet were set by means of a number of calculations. Availability was targeted at 85 per cent, a quantum leap from the 70–75 per cent being achieved at most BR DMU depots up until then, and typical of the radical thinking which accompanied Provincial's second director, John Edmonds. High-density seating with many rows fixed in face-to-back mode, together with much more standing room, enabled trains which had previously been formed of three old DMU vehicles to be scheduled for two Sprinter vehicles. Large tanks permitted the Sprinters to run longer (up to 1,000 miles) between the need to refuel, and maintenance visits to home depots were reduced from the two or three times weekly of older DMUs to fortnightly.

Thus was it possible for one new Sprinter vehicle to replace at least two old DMU coaches. In service the targets were beaten from day one. 90 per cent availability is now the norm, and there have been weeks when the 150/2 series, arguably the most reliable diesel trains ever to have run in Britain, have attained 100 per cent availability during the daytime. For not only is maintenance now much less frequent, all scheduled depot attention is given at night or at weekends or between peak diagrams. Thus, Sprinter units working out of Derby depot, covering as they did stopping services on routes spread out as far as Leeds, Manchester, Cambridge, Aberystwyth, Pwllheli, Holyhead, Scarborough, Skegness and Cleethorpes, actually achieved annual mileages in excess of 100,000 miles per year, practically double that achieved by the older DMUs.

Through the late 1980s another force was at work which turned the Provincial sector's fortunes further round. Increasing prosperity in the United Kingdom meant that people had more spare cash, and much of this was spent on an increase in personal travel. The new trains on the Provincial routes therefore had a market with a degree of positive elasticity not previously enjoyed. Inevitably the services which had been planned on the basis of high seat-load factors quickly became overcrowded. Provincial had been bitten by its own success.

Rediagramming of units, and the retention of old DMUs for many years longer than originally planned in order to keep up the fleet size to meet this new demand, have enabled the worst of the overcrowding to be contained, though there are at the time of writing (1989) still several tight spots to be dealt with in certain areas at peak times. And at the very end of the decade, after this chapter had been written, Provincial announced that such was the

Swindon Style. Still carrying its Trans-Pennine branding, four-car Class 124 dmu forms the 12.00 Leeds–Morecambe service near Clapham on 22 May 1982. These distinctive units were finally withdrawn in 1984.

96

Sprinter No 150279 – one of the 150/2 series built with gangwayed ends – in the Nantgarw Gap nearing Radyr on the Taff Vale main line. Castle Coch, a folly built on the site of a 13th century ruin by the Marquess of Bute, rises out of the wooded slopes in the background. 31 March 1988.

Class 45 1Co-Co1 No 45110 (withdrawn July 1988) skirts the Irish Sea near Penmaenmawr with an eight-coach Bangor–Newcastle train in August 1986. These services were brought in with the May 1983 timetable to improve the range of Trans-Pennine trains on offer. First-class accommodation is provided by an air-conditioned Mk2 coach, the most modern vehicle in the rake, second from the rear. The leading coach is a down-graded open first. Note the rockslide shelter (above the locomotive) protection from the granite quarries on the headland.

The European at Low Gill on its long journey south to Harwich Parkeston Quay. The motive power is provided by No 85013 as far as Preston, from where diesel traction will take over. The date is 9 August 1983, the service had commenced on the introduction of the summer timetable.

cost of retaining ageing DMUs that in 1990 some services would be temporarily reduced until more Sprinters come on stream.

If that all sounds like success, there is another, more amazing story which Provincial can now tell. And another one is just round the corner as this book is published. Following the success of the early Sprinters, which were basically of suburban body design and layout, later builds of Sprinter have been up-market, aimed at the longer-distance traveller. The Classes 155 (Leyland, Workington) and 156 (Metro-Cammell) employ longer, 23m bodies with end doors so that the central passenger saloon in each vehicle has the maximum possible space in which to arrange the medium-density seats. The

carriages are carpeted (whoever heard before of fully carpeted DMUs?), and the units have an ambience of comfort which is well matched by the refreshment-trolley service which is becoming the norm on the services on which these Super-Sprinters run.

What is really amazing however is the routes which have been dreamed up for the Super-Sprinters, and which have taken off with growth factors unbelieved when first disclosed. The process has evolved over the decade with the linking up of what used to be short runs into long, cross-country routes. Norwich–Birmingham had already been tried, with locomotive-hauled stock, but putting together the services which previously had separately linked

ScotRail push-pull Class 47/7 No 47716 Duke of Edinburgh's Award *(named July 1985) leaves Edinburgh Waverley with a shuttle service to Haymarket TMD for the ScotRail festival on 24 August 1985.*

Liverpool, Warrington Central, Manchester; Blackpool and Manchester; Sheffield via the Hope Valley line; Nottingham, Grantham, Peterborough, Ely and Ipswich/Norwich and Harwich Parkeston Quay, was a bold move from which has developed a popular route on which much new business is emerging.

Other new routes coming into fruition have included the welding together of the trans-Pennine services between Leeds and Manchester with those starting back at Newcastle, Scarborough, Hull and the main line to Liverpool, with connections to Chester and North Wales. There is also a route from Newcastle through Carlisle to Stranraer and/or Glasgow via Kilmarnock, which results from the combination of previously separate services. Most Super-Sprinter services are based on hourly or two-hourly clock-face timings, and a feature of their operation has been their reliability, much in the face of opposition from traditional railway operators who originally rejected out of hand the idea that end-on services could be linked up without transferring delays from one part of the system to another.

The next phase in the growth of the Provincial sector's services is the introduction of the new Class 158 units on the Sprinter Express routes. The 158 is a 90mph, fully air-conditioned DMU of high quality customer ambience specification. It is the nearest thing to a modern InterCity train, and yet has the flexibility and economy of the DMU. The quality is good enough to enable the 158s to replace the Mark 3 push-pull trains in Scotland as well as the Mark 2s. The 158s will revolutionise the trans-Pennine routes when they push the 156s away on to other lines. The annual mileages to be run by the new units will be well in excess of 150,000! Indeed, there is now a distinct possibility that the Provincial sector will create some profitable railway routes in its quest for efficiency and quality.

The Provincial story is still proceeding. Its present director is Sidney Newey, a successful career railwayman who sees almost endless possibilities for new routes. We shall have to wait until each is announced, but the possibility of reopening new routes – a far cry from bus substitution – raises a new image for the sector which ten years ago had been written off by some people as a collection of unremunerative passenger railways.

The key evidence of success is the financial results. From a frightening ratio of expenditure to fares revenue of four to one, the ratio has improved to better than two and a half to one and it is still improving.

8
CATERING

THE 1980s opened with British Transport Hotels (BTH) still running around thirty traditional railway hotels; with its Travellers-Fare wing sprucing up its portfolio of dull, old-fashioned refreshment rooms, and restaurant cars continuing to suffer declining patronage as journey times shortened and eating habits changed. The HSTs had effected one major positive change: an increase in hot snacks in the age of the microwave. The decade ended with the railway hotels not merely privatised but in many cases under second and third owners, generally poorer in standard and distinctly without the nation

Station Breakthrough: the first Casey Jones fast food restaurant, at Waterloo, seen here soon after its opening in October 1980.

having benefited (since they ran at a profit anyway), with Travellers-Fare privatised and healthier (both profitwise and in what they served), and with InterCity rethinking the role of the restaurant car and with many chefs still preparing meals on board.

It was in station catering, so long the Cinderella, that the changed order of the 1980s made its first mark. The fast-food revolution arrived in style in October 1980 with the opening of the first Casey Jones restaurant at Waterloo. Casey Jones, with its colourful, upbeat presentation, its production-line methods and its computer-controlled cooking, was light years away from anything seen before on British stations. Passengers and passers-by alike found its wide, illuminated photographs of mouth-watering meals irresistible – though at a cost (in 1980) of nearly £½million, Casey Jones was obviously going to pay for himself only at the busiest venues. Over the next five years the CJ chain grew to fourteen, including provincial cities such as Birmingham, Liverpool and Glasgow (Central and Queen Street), spawning meanwhile a revolution in approach throughout the business. The staff had been recruited and trained with a new professionalism; and the new methods now began spreading into the rest of station catering, bringing to the name Travellers-Fare a new credibility and respect. Marketing too underwent a revolution; old names – the 'Tournament' at Paddington, the 'Golden Frame' at Sheffield – were out, while in came the snappy new 'Quicksnack' or 'Station Tavern' that proudly proclaimed a new image nationwide.

Everywhere, too, customers were finding much nicer things to eat. Sandwiches – nearly 7 million sold on stations in 1985 – lost their 'curly' image; the new order was Tuna & Cucumber, Salami & Coleslaw, or BLT –

'Welcome Buffet' was a marketing attempt to jazz up the merchandising in the old Mk1 buffet cars, patently unsuited to the 1980s. Its success – unlike the public cynicism it generated – proved hard to identify.

bacon, lettuce and tomato. The immediate success of these fillings, and the brown bread they came in, reflected John Bull's broadening palate. As the 1980s progressed, seasoned travellers observed that the offerings of railway stations, airports and motorway service areas were growing more and more alike. All three are – or, in the case of railways, have become – essentially light catering markets; and in such markets profitability, the watchword of the times, calls for selling made-up products like plate meals or filled rolls, rather than retail lines like chocolate bars where the scope for mark-up is obviously small. It means, too, devoting as much space as possible to selling rather than seating.

All this had a dramatic effect on station catering's turnover, up from £33.1 million in 1978 to £62.8million seven years later. This was as well; for from 1980, the BR Property Board began charging Travellers-Fare a percentage of turnover, as rental; and if another retailer, caterer or not, could offer a better return, Travellers-Fare might find itself out.

One of the new-look business's greatest successes proved to be its Food Courts, where up to five takeaway counters open on to a central, supervised seating area. Euston, the first to open in July 1986, included 'Le Croissant Shop', a franchise business that at once complements and rivals Travellers-Fare. Its 'running powers' over TF territory reflected the rising political pressure to dilute, and ultimately privatise, all public sector businesses.

Under this nostrum, the more successful station catering became, the more saleable it was; and in May 1986, the threat of sell-off moved dramatically closer, when British Rail split Travellers-Fare into its train and station counterparts, train catering becoming an integral part of InterCity, with station catering, continuing under the name Travellers-Fare, as a totally self-standing business. Travellers-Fare had first been split out of BTH from 1 January 1982 as a preliminary to privatising the hotels.

This further split between train and station catering was rigidly enforced and led to some extremes of rivalry. One keen young steward on the Cannon Street–Hastings trains drummed up afternoon beer trade by operating his trolley on the platforms at Cannon Street. While trains are exempt from the licensing laws, stations are not. This was before the 1988 Licensing Act which brought all-day opening. A quick telephone call from the station's duty catering manager resulted in the young unfortunate being escorted for questioning by the heavy hand of the police.

In 1988 BR decided to sell station catering outright. That December, the Secretary of State for Transport announced the identity of the successful bidders: Travellers-Fare's own management. There was widespread pleasure at this, justice had been done. It had been a very different story with the earlier sell-off of the hotels where the managers' interest had not been shown proper respect.

No such satisfactory denouement came the way of the beleaguered train catering business. Political hotheads were demanding a sell-off; but no would-be purchaser dared tangle with the horrendous staff rostering costs, the problems of management control, the antiquated working conditions, the

The new dawn: Cuisine 2000 in its first month of service, August 1985, on the Euston–Manchester run.

railway operating hazards that frustrate a crew's best efforts while landing them with the blame and, not least, the ever-lurking cynicism of the media.

Unlocking all these problems needed several different keys. One of them was the mini-buffet, first introduced in 1980 on the Waterloo–Exeter run. Designed as a low-cost replacement for the fleet of 'miniature' buffet cars, then twenty years old, these trolleys were (and are) pre-loaded, operating on board from behind a small fixed counter in an open saloon coach. At any station en route the steward can speedily remove or exchange his trolley, or switch to another train. This highly flexible system quickly spread to long-distance commuter runs, such as Liverpool Street to Cambridge or Clacton; and in turn gave fresh impetus to the old dream of establishing corridor trolley services throughout the length of trains. The new, spacious Mk 3 rolling stock, with its luggage stowage space and automatic vestibule doors, was at last making these a practicality; and, despite some unofficial rearguard action, in 1984 the NUR ended opposition. The resulting at-seat light refreshment services provided an ideal foothold for the private operators whose involvement in railway catering the government was urging. The first of these now widespread services began, in the summer of 1984, between Chester and

106

Newport, run by Gylee Enterprises (whose 'operating manager' was a former Travellers-Fare station catering manageress).

The mini-buffets underlined anew the truism that if all food could somehow be prepared on terra firma, familiar restaurant-car hazards such as unreliable equipment and minuscule space would no longer matter. And technology was now offering a key to this problem also. Modern cook-chill processes, using liquid nitrogen, chill partly cooked food very rapidly to just above freezing point at which temperature it will keep perfectly for several days. Heating in a simple convection oven is all that remains to do on board; and this system, coupled with a range of basically similar ('modular') trolleys formed the basis of 'Cuisine 2000' begun experimentally between Euston and Manchester in August 1985. Modular catering cars retained an orthodox grill for that perennial favourite, the Great British Breakfast, which in 1987 accounted for 630,000 out of the total of 1.1 million main meals served.

Preparation of the food 'on shore' now offered private contractors a foothold in the core of the business, and this in turn led in 1987 to the highly symbolic step of privatising the railway sandwich. Once the butt of music-hall comics, the quality and range was further improved – and was an immediate success. Soon InterCity were claiming that sales had doubled to 5 million a year. Part of this somewhat free accounting was undoubtedly due to much better control: no longer could staff pass off a 'do-it-yourself' sandwich and pocket the proceeds; but much of the increase was real and deserved.

Cuisine 2000 itself, meanwhile, was enjoying a somewhat mixed reception. Freed from railborne restrictions, the new menus could offer much greater sophistication. Passengers now encountered 'Duckling in Ginger and Shallot Sauce: an irresistible combination of seasoned roasted duck, off the bone, served with a sauce of shallots, ginger, honey and white wine.' But such pretentious billing set up Cuisine 2000 for instant mockery whenever problems arose – as surely they did. Private contractors, appointed both to supply the food and to staff and run the 'shore' depots, seriously underestimated problems such as the relentless, unforgiving intensity of the railway timetable – very different from their airline experience where there are far more carpets under which to sweep catering delays. There were many complaints of altered menus, minuscule portions, and too often, of no food at all.

The running of Cuisine 2000 furthermore quickly proved very costly. Expensive bought-in food and increased depot costs were largely to blame. The forecast upsurge in takings did not happen. The cost of train catering to its parent BR Sector, InterCity, almost doubled between 1983 and 1988.

A review completed in spring 1989 confirmed once again the truths of the business: that catering is an essential and integral part of InterCity travel; that (trolleys excepted) most train catering, modular or otherwise, will ever be a net cost; and that therefore, the catering budget can only emerge after the extent and level of services have been specified. Setting a cost limit first, and then trying to tailor services to fit, causes only conflict and demoralisation.

So InterCity declared a policy for the 1990s of offering catering in some form, on all their services. Modular catering (though not necessarily Cuisine 2000) is expanding on to the Liverpool Street–Norwich run (using former West Coast vehicles), the East Coast main line (with Mk4 stock), and the Western Region, when the ex-ECML cars can be cascaded in 1991. Food will be bought-in at various stages of pre-preparation; but the operation of shorebases by contractors is at an end. Meal style and availability will vary, more than hitherto, with the journey length and passenger profile of each individual train.

Meantime BR's two other passenger sectors, Provincial and Network SouthEast, were left under the 1986 reorganisation without their own catering. Subsidies are out; if no one can operate their on-train catering profitably, then no catering there will be. Unlike at InterCity, little ticket revenue is considered at risk from taking this stance. Proper buffet cars are economic on only a small handful of their routes, notably Waterloo–Bournemouth. On many other routes, trolleys have provided an ideal low-cost solution and today's timetable shows a good variety of trains, including many of Provincial's Sprinter expresses.

Catering Chronology

21 October 1980	First Casey Jones fast-food restaurant opens, Waterloo station.
1 January 1982	Travellers-Fare (the combined train and station catering organisation) detached from British Transport Hotels to become a directly-controlled Division of British Rail.
14 May 1984	First privately run trolley catering begins, operated by Gylee Catering on Shrewsbury–Newport services.
25 November 1984	First Sunday Luncheon Special runs, from King's Cross to Norwich and back.
13 May 1985	Yorkshire Pullman and Merseyside Pullman introduced.
13 August 1985	Modular Catering launched, on Euston–Manchester.
26 August 1985	Catering headquarters moves from St Pancras Chambers to Tournament House, Paddington.
30 September 1985	Tees-Tyne Pullman introduced.
12 May 1986	Lancashire Pullman introduced.
26 May 1986	Train and station catering split: train catering becoming part of BR InterCity, station catering becoming self-standing but wholly owned division, continuing as Travellers-Fare.
27 June 1986	First Food Court opens, at Euston.
11 May 1987	Master Cutler and Birmingham Pullmans introduced. Manchester Pullman converted to Mk3B stock.
5 October 1987	Golden Hind Pullman introduced.
March/April 1988	21 Travellers-Fare locations transferred to private operation under competitive tendering exercise.
16 May 1988	Red Dragon and West Country Pullmans introduced. Peak District, Chester, and Stratford Pullmans on summer-season experimental basis.
20 December 1988	Travellers-Fare management buy-out announced.
15 May 1989	St David Pullman introduced.
20 September 1989	Mk4 catering vehicles launched on East Coast main line.

108

Among the first of the private trolley operators on BR were Rightline Caterers of Rhyl, seen here working the 17.40 Chester–Rhyl service on a very cold 25 February 1986, when the well-known instant coffee, common to both private and public sectors, was extremely welcome.

Hot Favourite: through the 1980s the Great British Breakfast took a larger and larger share of total main meals served. Mk2 first-class open vehicles, like that shown here, gave way to the Mk3 build, and glass jars of Cooper's Oxford Marmalade to plastic portion-sized containers.

9
FREIGHT, EVER MORE SPECIALIST

AT the beginning of the 1980s BR's freight business retained many facets of the inefficient, labour-intensive system of yesteryear. True, the 'Beeching era' of the 1960s had brought revolution in the form of Freightliner and unit trains, the latter represented above all by the highly successful 'merry-go-round' concept. But such innovations were only applied to certain traffic flows, and the old order of vacuum-braked or unfitted wagons, sprawling marshalling yards and generally lavish siding provision was allowed to linger on. It was only during the 1980s that it was finally laid to rest, enabling BR to run a fully modernised and streamlined freight system.

The most telling indicator of Railfreight's success in the 1980s was the unprecedented turnround in its financial performance. From a massive deficit of £281million in 1984–5, the year of the miners' strike, the sector was able to recover quickly to break-even point and then achieve a handsome surplus of £69million in 1988–9. In so doing Railfreight chalked up an achievement which would scarcely be considered feasible by any other European railway administration: only in Britain is the freight-carrying railway required to function without government subsidy.

Sectors and sub-sectors. Sectorisation had especially far-reaching consequences for Railfreight. Nothing has been allowed to stand in the way of the sector's progress towards profitability. It is free from many of the constraints of timetabling, shared usage of stations and so on which limit the extent of true independence amongst the passenger and parcels sectors. It has been able to shed its loss-making operations without the need for lengthy legal procedures such as those which normally accompany the proposal to close a branch passenger service. The further division of Railfreight into five sub-sectors, namely Coal, Construction, Petroleum, Metals and Distribution, has exposed the strengths and weaknesses of individual traffic flows and kept the degree of cross-subsidy within the sector to a minimum.

All the way through Railfreight's emergence as a viable, forward-looking concern, the emphasis was on improving the service to the customer. A bad reputation had resulted from years of unwieldy and sometimes inefficient management, coupled with the inherent un-reliability of the old wagonload system. Under sectorisation individual managers have much more clearly defined responsibility, and the need to keep the customer informed about the whereabouts of his goods, for example, is now recognised as paramount. An outward sign of Railfreight's resurgence was the brightly coloured livery which made its debut in October 1987. For locomotives there was now a livelier three-tone grey colour scheme with sub-sector logos and depot badges. Other Railfreight assets from office buildings to headed notepaper also received the appropriate embellishments.

The Railfreight Infrastructure. Railfreight is the sole user of numerous yards, sidings and terminals. Most running lines used by Railfreight are shared with at least one other sector, though there is a not insignificant mileage which exists purely for the benefit of freight. It is not surprising, then, that considerable rationalisation of yards, sidings, terminals and lines has taken place. To say that every inch of siding space must earn its keep by virtue of the traffic it carries is not so very far from the truth.

A striking example of rationalisation was the wholesale closure of the Severn Tunnel Junction marshalling yard complex in November 1987. The yard was a product of piecemeal development over many years and found an important role in the air-braked wagonload network (Speedlink) from the 1970s onwards. It was a convenient gathering point for all non-trainload traffic to and from South Wales, and also became the gateway to south-west England with feeder services to Bristol, Exeter, Plymouth and so on. Moreover it was not an under-used white elephant in the manner of Kingmoor yard in Carlisle; traffic levels remained comparatively healthy right up to the

Railfreight Petroleum's new image. Refurbished Class 37/7 No 37888 Petrolea *passes Stratford with the 09.22 Micheldever–Ripple Lane empty tank train on 3 November 1988. The high-capacity wagons would be worked to one of the refineries at Thames Haven. The North Thameside petroleum traffic was among the first to have its own train crew and dedicated fleet of locomotives.*

Laira-based Class 37s. No 37672 Freight Transport Association *(in old Railfreight livery) and No 37673 (in new two-tone grey) pass Cockwood Harbour, near Exeter, with the 15.45 St Blazey to Gloucester freight on 17 August 1989.*

end. In their quest to reduce costs, however, the Railfreight managers were keen to explore every way of streamlining their operations, and in the case of Severn Tunnel Junction it was found that total closure would bring substantial savings for relatively little inconvenience. Most of the work previously carried out at Severn Tunnel Junction was transferred to Gloucester, Cardiff Tidal and East Usk (Newport) yards, with Stoke Gifford (Bristol) playing a minor role. Though in the early days there were capacity problems at Gloucester, by and large the new arrangements have worked well.

Many other yards throughout the BR network saw reductions in activity as a result of the continued trend towards unit or 'block' train working. Toton was a pivotal Speedlink yard in 1980 but its status had been reduced to that of staging and storage sidings, plus a small amount of household coal shunting, by the end of the decade. The importance of Healey Mills yard (West Yorkshire) has declined in a similar way, with most of its shunting duties transferred to Tinsley (Sheffield) and Doncaster. But two entirely new yards were opened towards the end of the decade, showing that BR envisages at least some need for shunting for the foreseeable future! These yards are both in South Wales, at Margam and Ebbw Vale. Both were sponsored by

112

the Metals sub-sector for specific categories of traffic, rather than by Railfreight Distribution for general Speedlink work.

So far as terminals are concerned, the trend of the 1980s has been overwhelmingly towards the setting up of private distribution depots, so running down BR's own facilities. The traditional railway goods depot, with its acres of sidings and its own cranage and cartage facilities, has declined almost to the point of extinction. Some towns and cities are now devoid of any kind of public freight terminal, or even a suitable siding which could be used for a one-off consignment. Where private enterprise has stepped in, the results have been variable. Among the more successful privately owned terminals have been the Glaswegian trio of Deanside, Mossend and Law Junction, all of which (but especially the first two) have attracted healthy quantities of regular traffic. More specialised terminals, such as those handling chemicals or coal, have thrived in relation to the industry they serve, though the tendency has been to close lesser used depots whenever investment in new track or pointwork has become necessary. Most of the new terminals commissioned during the 1980s were funded partly by the government by means of a 'Section 8 Grant', giving up to 60 per cent of the total cost.

As for running lines, the axe fell principally on two categories of 'freight only' railway: through lines where an adequate diversionary route existed; and branch lines which carried only small quantities of wagonload traffic. Casualties in the first category included Walsall–Brownhills, the Woodhead route, Northampton–Market Harborough, Warrington–Skelton, Bottesford–Newark and Airdrie–Bathgate. Examples of the second category are Wymondham–Dereham/Ryburgh, Barnstaple–Torrington/Meeth, Grimsby–Louth, Perth–Forfar and Kinnaber–Brechin. Where a rural freight branch has survived, this is only because of the presence of a major user, such as Blue Circle Cement at Eastgate, Associated Octel at Amlwch and Esso at Fawley. Such branch lines are of course vulnerable to changes in output level or distribution policy of their users. The Staffordshire branches to Caldon Low and Oakamoor were each carrying several trainloads of aggregates a week in the mid 1980s but their traffic was lost to road transport in 1988 and 1989 respectively. Sometimes the closure of a through 'freight only' route and the consequent diversion of traffic fails to bring the desired results. While the costs of maintaining the closed route will be saved, these may be offset by the need to deploy additional resources because of the extra time required to send trains via the diversionary route. This phenomenon occurred twice in the 1980s: Dee Marsh–Mickle Trafford was closed in 1984 but reopened mainly for steel coil traffic in 1986, and Annbank–Mauchline closed in 1985 but came back into use as a Railfreight Coal asset in 1988. In the case of Annbank–Mauchline, the reopening allowed an enhanced schedule of Knockshinnoch–Ayr coal trains to be covered by one pair of locomotives instead of two.

Bulk Traffic. Four out of the five Railfreight sub-sectors deal mainly with bulk traffic which travels by the trainload rather than by the individual wagonload. Few would deny that the railway is admirably suited to carrying this type of traffic. So as the 1980s drew to a close, the sub-sectors dubbed Coal, Construction, Petroleum and Metals were all in fine shape, and their outlook for the 1990s is promising. Not that the eighties were without their problems: quite apart from the industrial recession of the early years, which affected all Railfreight's bulk traffics to some degree or other, there was the historic miners' strike of 1984–5, taking heavy toll of steel as well as coal carryings. Happily the coal traffic was revived to the point where pre-strike tonnages were exceeded, although the number of individual collieries served was vastly reduced. The 'merry-go-round' system which allows loading and discharge to take place while an entire train remains in motion has continued to form the mainstay of Railfreight Coal's operations, and it is difficult to imagine a more efficient alternative.

Railborne steel traffic suffered in proportion to the cutbacks in the steel industry itself, with complete withdrawal from one or two locations such as Consett in County Durham. Interestingly, though, Railfreight also derived some benefit from the contraction of British Steel's steel-making activities. The concentration of blast furnaces at a smaller number of plants meant that the rolling mills at Corby and Shotton, for example, would henceforth receive their raw steel from other parts of the country. This provided Railfreight with valuable contracts for long-distance bulk coil traffic, traffic which would not have materialised if the steel industry had survived the 1980s unscathed. Another area of growth within the Metals sub-sector has been finished 'bright steel' or cold reduced coil. Almost non-existent at the beginning of the 1980s, rail carryings of this commodity had assumed significant proportions by the end of the decade, showing Railfreight both eager and able to adapt to new opportunities.

The Petroleum sub-sector began the decade in the doldrums, having lost much of its traffic due to reduced demand and surrendered further flows to long-distance pipelines. An upturn in tonnages was recorded in the latter part of the decade, however, and the threat of at least one further pipeline receded when Total Oil renewed a major contract with BR in 1988. As for Railfreight Construction, the transporting of bulk aggregates from quarries such as Merehead and Whatley has thrived unabated, particularly to London and the South East where the construction industry's appetite could no longer be satisfied from local sources. A record quantity of 14 million tonnes was carried in 1987–8, of which over three-quarters were destined for the South East. Twenty years previously this traffic had amounted to just two million tonnes per annum. Also worthy of mention for the Construction sub-sector is the growth in domestic waste traffic. By the late 1980s regular trainloads were being dispatched from purpose-built transfer terminals in Greater London, Manchester and Avon, and these would soon be joined by a new flow from Edinburgh.

The Distribution Problem. Railfreight's success in the 1980s was clouded by one area of uncertainty. That was the non-bulk wagonload operation, later

marketed as Railfreight Distribution. The basic problem remained, as always, the cost of providing a service to a large number of individual freight terminals, many receiving only a handful of wagons each week. On the positive side, a milestone was reached in 1984 when the old vacuum-braked wagonload network was finally abandoned and all worthwhile traffic transferred to the air-braked Speedlink system. The principle of Speedlink is that train sections are exchanged at specified groups of sidings on the network, rather than individual wagons sorted at full-scale marshalling yards. On certain routes Speedlink has served BR and its customers well, with many trunk trains running to capacity; but the economics of running three-or four-wagon feeder services at the periphery of the network have remained questionable. Some worthwhile traffic gains were made during the 1980s, such as timber from the Scottish Highlands and drinks from several locations in the South West. But equally notable were the losses, such as the once substantial Rowntrees traffic from York. Nor was the Distribution balance sheet improved by the abstraction of most coal and steel traffic from Speedlink services, in 1986–7 and 1989 respectively, to form dedicated networks for these commodities.

Towards the end of the decade Railfreight Distribution was increasingly

Old style wagonload marshalling. The down sorting sidings at Tees Yard are pictured from the hump control tower on 12 September 1980, with Class 08 pilot No 08770 in attendance. The yard looks busy, but close examination reveals that very few of the wagons were carrying traffic. The hump was closed in 1985 and all shunting carried out from the east end.

115

Railfreight's greatest success – Coal by merry-go-round. Class 58 No 58026 approaches Moira West Junction on the freight-only Burton-Leicester line, with a rake of empty HAAs from Drakelow power station on 30 October 1986, bound for Bagworth opencast loading point. The importance of the Leicestershire coalfield declined during the 1980s as seams gradually became worked out, but new opencast sites continued to provide useful revenue for BR.

setting its sights on traffic between Britain and mainland Europe as a major source of revenue. Until 1987 there were two separate train ferry operations for through freight traffic between Britain and the continent, Dover–Dunkerque and Harwich–Zeebrugge. This arrangement was, however, in many ways inefficient, and in January 1987 the Harwich–Zeebrugge service was withdrawn and all train ferry traffic routed via Dover. In the short term this did result in a reduction in capacity, leading many observers to criticise BR for short-sightedness in view of the need to attract new traffic in readiness for the opening of the Channel Tunnel, but during 1988 the Dover–Dunkerque service received a boost when Railfreight Distribution commissioned a new high-capacity ferry, the *Nord – Pas de Calais*, to cater both for individual wagonload consignments and for trainload traffic on this route. This enables Railfreight to cater for a modest increase in international traffic in the years leading up to the opening of the Channel Tunnel.

Another change which took place with the anticipated increase in continental traffic in mind was the merger of Railfreight Distribution with the former BRB subsidiary Freightliners Ltd in 1988. This allowed BR to concentrate all its non-bulk freight activities under one organisation, and eliminated the counter-productive competition which might otherwise occur between Freightliner and the conventional wagonload (ie Speedlink) network. By 1989 there was only one regular instance of Speedlink and Freightliner traffic sharing the same train, this being a service between Bristol and Coatbridge, but the organisation had already begun marketing its two products as complementary rather than competing systems, itself an important step forward in the history of Railfreight.

Traction Developments. Now that all three passenger sectors prefer unit trains to the traditional combination of locomotive and coaches, the Railfreight sector is left as the prime user of diesel locomotives. Mixed-traffic types such as the Brush Class 47 have fallen from favour since they inevitably entail a compromise between a high maximum speed for passenger working and a high tractive effort for freight haulage.

Bulk freight in Wensleydale. The twenty-three-mile branch line from Northallerton has survived only because of the Tarmac quarry terminal located at Redmire, supplying limestone for use as a flux in the steel-making process. Class 47 No 47302 passes Ainderby with the 10.12 up train on 8 August 1986, hauling 900 tonnes of limestone in privately owned PGA wagons. It is common practice nowadays to introduce guard-operated level crossings on rural freight-only lines.

The only orders for new diesel locomotives placed during the 1970s and 1980s, were for locomotives designed specifically to haul freight. First came the Class 56, superficially similar to the Class 47 but with a maximum speed of 80mph and no facility for train heating. A fleet of 135 Class 56 locomotives was introduced between 1977 and 1984. Next came the Class 58, functionally similar to the Class 56 but with a number of radical design features such as external walkways along the sides of each locomotive; a fleet of fifty entered service between 1984 and 1987. And as the 1980s drew to a close, the first locomotives of Class 60 were rolling out of the Brush works at Loughborough, destined to become the standard Railfreight traction unit well into the early years of the twenty-first century. Perhaps the most exciting new build of the 1980s, however, was the small fleet of Class 59 locomotives built for Foster Yeoman of Merehead in Somerset. Not only were these the first privately owned diesels to regularly haul freight trains over BR main lines,

116

but they were also remarkable in having originated at La Grange, Illinois. So successful was the Class 59, perhaps embarrassingly so from the viewpoint of British manufacturers, that the initial order for four machines was followed up by orders for five more, comprising one for additional Foster Yeoman traffic and four for the neighbouring but rival firm ARC.

Existing traction resources were trimmed severely as the new, more efficient types entered service. Less favoured designs such as Classes 25, 40 and 45 were withdrawn completely, and the Railfreight sector relinquished its claim on the costly Class 50. A major life-extension programme was carried out on nearly half the Class 37 fleet, with a number of variants designed specifically for freight haulage and expected to survive into the next century.

Some important changes were made to maintenance arrangements, whereby locomotives became attached first and foremost to specific traffic flows rather than to a defined geographical area. Many diesel depots ceased to carry out maintenance for the Railfreight sector, with some facing the axe such as Gateshead and others concentrating on work for other sectors such as Bristol Bath Road. Out of the thirteen which still had a formal Railfreight allocation in 1989, many had become specialised bases for traction belonging to a particular sub-sector. Toton and Tinsley are good examples of depots with specific sub-sector allegiances and covering a wide geographical area. Toton took over responsibility for all Railfreight Coal traction used in the Midlands, North West, Yorkshire and North East districts, comprising some 250 locomotives of Classes 20, 56 and 58. Tinsley became the base for over

Foster Yeoman's 126 tonne Co-Co Class 59 No 59004 Yeoman Challenger *passing West Ealing with the 10.05 Acton Yard to Merehead empty stone hoppers on 13 August 1988.*

150 locomotives used on Speedlink services throughout the BR network, comprising members of Classes 31, 37 and 47. At the other end of the scale, Plymouth Laira gained a small fleet of Class 37s which rarely ventured away from the West Country china clay empire, although a new trainload working was introduced in 1989 which would take them twice a week up to Irvine in South West Scotland. At some maintenance depots the establishment of specific sub-sector pools led to significant improvements to reliability, even though in many cases the locomotives concerned were travelling further from home than ever before. The only Railfreight traction to retain common-user status was the AC electric fleet on the West Coast main line.

Wagons. The number of wagons used on BR continued to shrink dramatically during the 1980s. In 1979 there were over 150,000 vehicles authorised for main-line running, but by 1989 the total had fallen to around 40,000. Over the same period BR's annual freight tonnage fell only marginally, from 169 million tonnes to 149 million tonnes, so the reduction in size of the wagon

Coal in the valleys. The number of rail-served collieries in South Wales declined dramatically in the 1980s. Class 37 No 37234 pulls forward through the disused station at Tondu on 15 April 1982, having just run round its train of MDVs carrying coal from Garw to Ogmore. By 1989 the branches from Tondu to Garw and Ogmore had both closed, leaving only Maesteg as a source of traffic in this once thriving part of the Welsh coalfield.

No 37109 brings a freight off the Dundee line through platform No 1 at Perth station on 8 September 1987.

fleet was a remarkable achievement. The main casualties were railway-owned vehicles fitted with vacuum brakes or with no automatic brake at all. Many such wagons spent long periods hidden away in marshalling yards or being used as storage containers on customers' premises, practices which the business-led Railfreight sector was understandably keen to eradicate.

The new vehicles built as replacements during the 1980s were generally of higher capacity, privately owned and fitted with air brakes. Where a customer did not wish to purchase his own fleet of wagons, he was usually encouraged to hire or lease from firms such as Procor or Tiphook in preference to using railway-owned vehicles. In the Construction sub-sector, for example, the use of railway-owned vehicles on aggregates traffic ceased altogether in 1989, following the withdrawal of a pool of 16.5 tonne opens based in the Peak District. Almost half of the serviceable BR-owned wagon fleet in 1989 comprised 'merry-go-round' coal hoppers, with the remainder consisting largely of steel carriers, some vans and opens for general merchandise traffic, and – rather surprisingly and after much argument with the industry – the fleet of china clay carriers built to replace the venerable 'clay hoods' in 1988.

Towards the end of the 1980s attention was being focussed on some interesting developments in wagon design. The MiniLink and MaxiLink container systems, both of which appeared in 1987, incorporated some novel design features which enabled road-rail transfer without the need for separate lifting equipment. An even more exciting development was TrailerTrain, comprising a specially profiled road trailer which could be loaded on to railway bogies, again without the need for fixed equipment at the transfer location. Finally, one of the best kept secrets of the decade until its unveiling in 1988 was the Redland self-discharge aggregates train, a permanently coupled set of hopper wagons with a conveyor belt running underneath and a special unloading vehicle at one end.

Railfreight in the 1980s – A Chronology

Mar 1980	Railfreight loses £30million due to steel strike.
May 1980	Official opening of new Freightliner terminal at Seaforth, Liverpool.
Oct 1980	Port Talbot–Llanwern ore trains, heaviest on BR, increased to 3,300 tonnes gross.
Oct 1980	Maximum Freightliner raised to 30 wagons due to increasing maritime traffic.

Pick-up goods on the Midland main line. Class 25 No 25303 draws to a halt at Finedon Road, Wellingborough, with an up local trip working on 1 July 1981. At this time BR's wagon fleet comprised an awkward mixture of vacuum-braked and air-braked vehicles, making the brake van an essential feature of many wagonload services. The train has a vacuum-braked fitted head, one VVV van and two HTV hoppers, but the air-braked OBA wagons at the rear are running with their automatic brakes inoperative.

Jul 1981	Woodhead route closes; trans-Pennine freight lost or diverted.
May 1982	Whitemoor marshalling yard rationalised.
Dec 1982	First Class 58 locomotive delivered.
Jan 1983	Serpell Report on railway finances published; customer confidence is dented as doubts arise about future of BR system.
May 1983	Speedlink Distribution launched.
May 1983	All wagonload traffic except coal and scrap transferred to Speedlink.
May 1983	End of through freight traffic on Settle & Carlisle line.
Sep 1983	New coal link built from Coedbach to Kidwelly against a trend of major cutbacks in South Wales.
Mar 1984	11 month long miners' strike starts; much coal, steel and ore traffic lost.
May 1984	Demise of vacuum-braked wagonload network.
May 1984	Acton marshalling yard closes.
Jul 1984	Atomic flask withstands 100mph impact in a spectacular staged demonstration.
Jul 1984	Metals landmark: 2,000th Lackenby–Workington slab train.
Oct 1984	Distribution landmark: 150th Speedlink service inaugurated.
Nov 1984	Last of 135 Class 56 locomotives delivered.
Dec 1984	Tinsley yard drastically rationalised.
Feb 1985	Last Class 40 locomotive withdrawn from normal revenue-earning service.
Jan 1986	Four Foster Yeoman Class 59 locomotives arrive from General Motors, USA.
Jan 1986	£12million coal terminal opened at Tyne Dock.
Feb 1986	First of Railfreight's life-extended Class 37s goes on trial.
Feb 1986	Trials with Class 59s presage BR's heaviest trains: 4,692 tonnes gross Merehead–Acton.
Sep 1986	Dudley Freightliner terminal closes; 9 more terminals follow suit in 1986/7.
Sep 1986	Mickle Trafford–Dee Marsh line reopens 2 years after closure.
Nov 1986	Tiphook Rail Ltd will spend £10million on new wagons for hire to BR customers.
Jan 1987	Rowntrees traffic lost; closure of York Dringhouses yard ensues.
Jan 1987	Harwich–Zeebrugge train ferry withdrawn; all traffic now via Dover.
Mar 1987	New link opens from Trimley to Felixstowe North Freightliner terminal.
Mar 1987	Last of 50 Class 58 locomotives delivered.
Mar 1987	Final stage of Speedlink Coal Network implemented.
Mar 1987	Last Class 25 locomotive withdrawn.
Oct 1987	New Railfreight sub-sector liveries unveiled at Ripple Lane.
Feb 1988	Cornish 'clay hoods' replaced by air-braked rolling stock.
May 1988	Contract signed for construction of 100 Class 60 locomotives.
May 1988	New high-capacity train ferry enters service on Dover–Dunkerque route.
Oct 1988	Freightliner becomes part of Railfreight Distribution.
Mar 1989	Railfreight achieves its best results of the decade: a £64.9million operating surplus.
Jun 1989	First Class 60 leaves Brush factory at Loughborough.
Oct 1989	Major reorganisation of Speedlink flows commences; Network 90 foreshadowed.

No 37011, with Ethel heating unit No 97251, hauls the overnight sleeper from London (Euston) near Torlundy on the last stage of its journey to Fort William. The photograph is dated 24 April 1984 and shows the development of BR stock up to that date in the make-up of the rake. The leading vehicle is a Mk1 open brake second fitted with a micro buffet area (B1 bogies) followed by Mk2 vehicles, both early and later air-conditioned examples carried on B4 bogies, finally two Mk3A sleeping cars built in the early 1980s with BT10 bogies.

10
COACHES

AT the beginning of the 1980s passengers experienced great variances of comfort and style on InterCity and cross-country trains mainly according to whether they were travelling in one of the three basic designs that made up most of the fleet, one each from the fifties, sixties and seventies. Features dating from before World War I were still commonly encountered, along with luxury wall-to-wall carpeting even in what today we call standard class. Side corridors and composite vehicles (for example first and standard or first and guard's van) were still common.

They were the days when many passengers were afraid to enter a second-class compartment believing (because of its quality) it must be a first, of a mixture of vacuum and air-braked stock, steam and electric heating, and continual development and changes with the design of bogies. The Mark 2 coaches inaugurated in 1966 had generally set a new standard of comfort with for example better heating and ventilation but there were no Mark 2 catering or sleeping cars. So a familiar sight of the early 1980s was a standard formation of Mark 2 vehicles with an obviously inferior Mark 1 catering vehicle squeezed in. The production of Mark 3 vehicles, at first for the High Speed

Mk2A open second No E5259 as built at Derby in 1967. The Mk2As featured integral construction and were fitted with air brake and dual heating facilities (steam now isolated). The internal layout is similar to the Mk1 with two lavatories at the same end of the vehicle.

Trains, began in 1975, but the proportion of even top-grade express trains composed of them in the early 1980s was still small.

The HSTs were important from several points of view, not least because they marked the beginning of the end of the once strict division between locomotive-hauled and self-propelled stock. The story of the HSTs power-wise does not belong here but from the point of view of passenger comfort we should note that while much was conventional there was also much that was new . . . though not so revolutionary as to require years of testing and modification (and run the risk of ultimate rejection as in the case of the Advanced Passenger Train).

The integral construction of bodies, new air-sprung bogies, air conditioning, excellent sound and heat insulation, and a high standard of luxury furnishing and decor for both second and first class, and above all strength to resist compression and buckling forces in an accident to an extent never seen before, brought a new era to BR coach design and made the HSTs deservedly popular. Even their automatically operated doors at their ends were widely appreciated. A variation known as Mark 3A was produced for locomotive haulage, differing only in having side buffers available when necessary, and centre buck-eye couplers instead of the special couplers on the 125 sets, and electric wiring to suit the different needs of locomotive haulage.

The remarkable feature of the Mark 3 is the fact that only one basic bodyshell was produced so that standard-class coaches have exactly the same external dimensions, window spacing and appearance as the first class. There is, though, one large disadvantage that became much discussed in the eighties: standard-class seats do not match the window spacing. For every four windows on a Mark 3 standard-class coach there are four and a half bays of seats, only the end bays matching the windows and succeeding bays being more tightly spaced so that some passengers are seated against a blank wall. But in riding, quietness, and general environment, Mark 3 coaches gliding through the countryside at speed owe little to even a decade ago. Wall-to-wall carpeting, luggage racks running lengthways above the windows, supplemented by space for cases and bags between the seats, provide an uncluttered spaciousness to give a relaxed atmosphere on the longest of journeys.

At least that is what it should be like. The upsurge in traffic in the 1980s has alas meant that passengers have often had to stand in the centre aisles, in the lobbies, and around the door vestibules. With floor sensors operating the automatic sliding doors between the end vestibules and the passengers' saloons perpetually energised by standing passengers, travel in an over-crowded Mark 3 coach seems little better than its predecessors.

Mk3A (loco hauled) tourist open second No M12004 carried on BT10 bogies. This coach received Provincial ScotRail livery during the 1980s and worked in push-pull rakes from Edinburgh Craigentinny depot.

At the upper end of luxury the first-class Mark 3s have much more room with one-plus-two seating, like their earlier Mark 1 and 2 counterparts but all in open saloon accommodation, since the side-corridor coach was deemed to be a thing of the past. Even Mrs Thatcher levelled criticism at the lack of compartment privacy, but the policy against compartments was now firmly established.

The 1980s ended very differently from their beginning. For a start, each

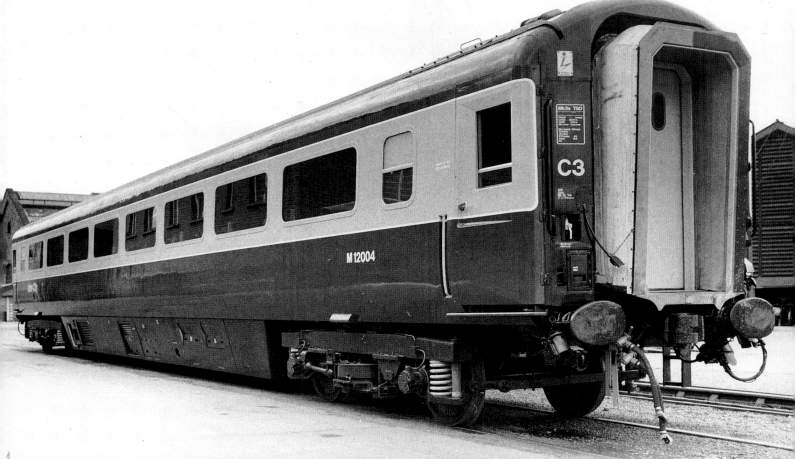

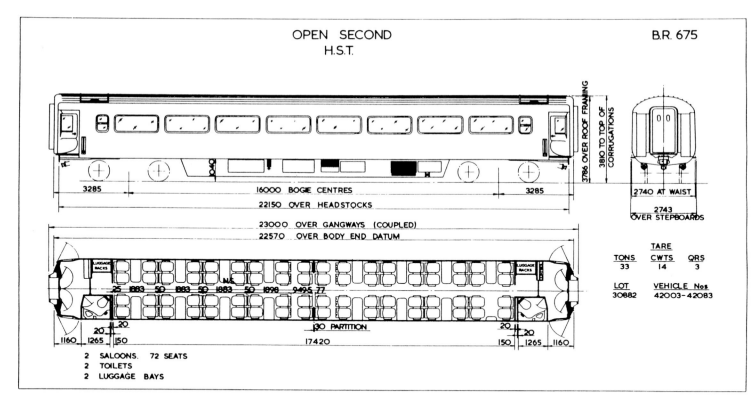

OPEN SECOND
H.S.T.

B.R. 675

2 SALOONS.   72 SEATS
2 TOILETS
2 LUGGAGE BAYS

The standard Mk3 open second as built with tables for four apart from the twin face-to-back seats at the centre partition. Because the second-class coaches use a common bodyshell with first-class coaches, seats do not always align with windows.

of the sectors has its distinctive livery, though much of the old corporate blue-and-grey still survived into 1990. InterCity of course has its light and dark grey with a red band under the windows, while Scotrail established its own blue band instead of red. Network South East has its patriotic red, white, and blue bands with grey thrown in for good measure. The PTEs sport their own colour schemes on a variety of multiple units.

As for Provincial, if you were visiting an area in which you were not quite sure what to expect, you might find Mark 1 or 2 (the latter air conditioned or otherwise) locomotive-hauled rakes of various lengths and compositions, first-generation multiple units (anything from one to nine cars, riding roughly but still with forward and rear vision), or the latest Sprinters, plain, super or express, many with privately run buffet-trolley service on long cross-country journeys.

On the main line, the remorseless reduction in fleet sizes resulted in Mark 3 vehicles steadily being more predominant. But at the end of 1989 Mark 2s were still well in evidence (particularly the air-conditioned types) and Mark 1 coaches will still be found on occasional reliefs or specials as well as some daily Network SouthEast locomotive-hauled services (especially out of Paddington) for some time to come.

During the decade new Mark 3 pattern sleeping cars were evolved at long last to replace the Mark 1s. They incorporated all the Mark 3 features of air conditioning, insulation and good riding. But they were just at the design stage when early on a July morning in 1978 twelve passengers died in a fire on Mark 1 sleeping cars of the Penzance to Paddington overnight train. As a result the design was modified to include much greater fire resistance, adding £50,000 per car to the basic cost of £200,000 of the initial design. So far it has not been put to the test in service. But Mark 3 stock in its conventional form has been involved in accidents, and has been found to stand up with little crushing and buckling in potentially horrific situations where in older stock casualties might have been high. Probably the most outstanding demonstration of their strength was in the 100mph Colwich collision in 1986 when despite coaches – some of them Mark 2s but largely Mark 3s – being piled on top of each other, or spreadeagled across the track, not a single passenger was killed.

Safe as the Mark 3 coaches have been, however, their designers have been responsible for actually causing one or two accidents because straps and fixings holding underfloor equipment were inadequate and worked loose, allowing major items to fall off. The worst case was in July 1989 when an alternator set fell off at around 100mph at Harrow on the main line into Euston and caused a major derailment, fortunately with no more than a few injuries.

As the decade concluded the Mark 4 coach arrived (at first on the East Coast newly electrified service to Leeds). A development of the Mark 3, it contains some APT features including a curved narrowing body profile which would allow the body to tilt like the APT but which feature is now unlikely to be used. Like the Mark 3s, the Mark 4s have a lightweight steel body (but there is simpler framing for ease of construction). The bogies are new: the BT41 evolved in Switzerland, to give good riding at the 140mph (225 km/hr) speeds for which these coaches have been designed.

From the passenger's viewpoint the first things that are different are the plug-type sliding doors, improved welcoming entrance vestibules and a seating layout with some facing pairs of seats in the standard class at tables for four, with others in twos having a face-to-back arrangement. Like the Mark 3s with an identical window spacing for standard- and first-class coaches this gets over much, but not all, of the criticisms of seats alongside blank panels between windows. The doors between end vestibules and saloons are now controlled by push buttons instead of floor sensors, but how do you press the button if both hands are carrying luggage or a tray meal from the buffet? Decor and furnishing are for the 1990s styles, insulation is even better than the Mark 3s and passengers with special needs are catered for as, for example, mother and baby facilities and disabled toilets. The first-class saloon is visually broken in two, less tube-like, the gangway's position changing half way through.

Plans evolved for new trains for the 1990s Channel Tunnel workings between British provincial centres and Paris, Brussels, and beyond being formed into eighteen coach trains with a power car at each end like an extended electric version of the InterCity 125 diesels, but with the capability to split into nine-coach trains push-pull style with a single power car, perhaps they are all things to all men. Maybe the purely locomotive-hauled coach could be obsolete or at least an enthusiast's treasure by the end of the nineties.

BR Standard Coaches Running in the 1980s

Type	Built	Length (over headstocks)	Remarks
Basic Mark 1	1951–64	63ft 5in	Separate underframe
Prototype Mark 2	1963	64ft	Integral construction Mark 1 style interior
XP64 Prototypes	1964	63ft 5in	New layouts and decor Separate underframe
Mark 2 production	1965–7	64ft	Vacuum braked, integral construction
Mark 2a	1967	64ft	Air braked
Mark 2b	1968	64ft	Wrap-round end doors, centre doors eliminated, reduced seating in open seconds
Mark 2c	1969	64ft	Designed for later fitting of air conditioning, but not carried out
Mark 2d	1970	64ft	Air conditioned
Mark 2e	1971	64ft	Fluorescent lighting, and 64 seats in open seconds (as Mark 2a) restored
Mark 2f	1973	64ft	Mark 3 style seating
Mark 3 prototype High Speed Diesel Train	1972	72ft 8in	
Mark 3 Production HST	1975	72ft 8in	
Mark 3a	1975	72ft 8in	Locomotive-hauled
Mark 3b	1985	72ft 8in	Open first and Pullman
Mark 4	1989	74ft	Sliding plug doors and many detailed improvements from Mark 3

Delivery of the Mk4s from Metro-Cammell commenced in 1989. Initially for the East Coast route they include disabled and mother-and-baby facilities. Marginally longer than the Mk3s at 23m over body, the bodysides incline inwards slightly to allow for tilting on curves, a feature not fitted, but noticeable in this view of a standard-class interior.

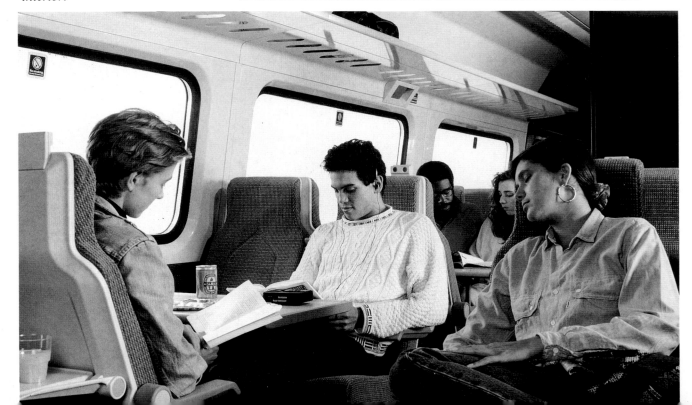

11
CLOSURES
AND OPENINGS

SUCH has been the scale of reopenings (not to mention survivals) of lines and stations in the 1980s that to put matters in perspective it is necessary to go back a bit in history.

Closures of railway lines had been taking place for many years, accelerated by the growing availability of cars in the 1950s. The upsurgence of the motor car was forcibly rammed home when the cross-country holiday route, the Midland & Great Northern Joint line from Peterborough across Norfolk to Great Yarmouth Beach station was shut on 28 February 1959.

Dr Beeching's famous report of January 1963 then opened the floodgates

Closure and Opening. Six-car Metro-Cammell dmu arrives at South Shields with a service from Newcastle in April 1980. The station was closed to BR trains when it became part of the Tyne & Wear Metro system.

to closure proposals, battles by campaigners and, invariably, consent by the Conservative Government which, after all, was the architect behind Dr Beeching's appointment as Chairman charged with reducing losses.

Throughout the 1960s and 1970s, line after line closed. Many were main or arterial routes. Some were duplicated by other routes, a legacy of the pre-Grouping days (1923) when companies competed for business. (If ever there was a lesson to be learnt in today's world, competition definitely did not work!) Giants like the Great Central Railway – in latter days known by its despairing appreciators as the Gone Completely Railway – and the Leeds Northern main line north of Harrogate, through Ripon, were two such casualties. Scores of branch lines closed despite the economies of diesel traction. Even the introduction of four-wheeled railbuses in the early 1960s failed to stem the closures.

By the time 1970 dawned, the closures were beginning to slow down. Public opinion was becoming more concentrated. Closure battles were more embittered and MPs had to take notice. Closures had practically ceased by 1980 but a far greater force had by then begun to take effect. The formation of the Metropolitan County Councils and their respective Passenger Transport Authorities would begin to have a far reaching effect on the future of many lines and stations.

With a background of socialism, these PTAs were not averse to spending public money on promoting public transport. Rail began to benefit. At first, it appeared an anachronism for BR to go to a council and say, 'please give us some money to build a new station' or, 'we need a subsidy to keep this service going'. Many councils were sceptical. Some are to this day. Many took the plunge and the great rail revival had started.

The seven PTAs – Sir Peter Parker called them 'The Magnificent Seven' – have been the driving force behind scores of new initiatives to improve rail services by building new stations – often replacing ones closed by Dr Beeching – restoring passenger services to freight-only lines and, incredibly, in the case of the West Yorkshire PTA actually purchasing their own trains!

Yet at the end of the eighties the only government money paid to BR was the rapidly dwindling subsidy paid to Provincial and Network SouthEast sectors to support loss-making services and talk continued of 'bustitution', however ridiculed it was by professional transport executives. The broader view based on cost benefit analysis (taking all costs and benefits into account) was still unacceptable to a government insisting on an 8 per cent direct investment return.

Thus, unless some sympathetic council contributes to a station or reopened line, improvements will not happen. The classic example of the inequality faced by BR was at Dornoch on the line between Inverness and Wick/Thurso. The new road bridge spanning the Dornoch Firth was suggested as having a dual role – carrying both road and rail, the rail section to be a new piece of line which would cut out a long detour and dramatically reduce the journey time to the Far North. The cost of the rail link was a paltry £12million and all but three million pounds had been found elsewhere. The Scottish Office

still refused to pay this £3million despite the astronomic sums spent on the parallel A9 road.

One area which saw a great revival in rail fortunes is South Wales where local and county councils invested public money – and reaped the rewards. At the end of 1988, BR's Provincial sector announced that the Valley Lines had doubled their revenue in five years, the only Provincial services to do so! The ultimate achievement, notwithstanding the numerous new stations opened in the area during the last five years, was the reopening to passenger traffic of the Cynon Valley line to Aberdare (closed in March 1964) with no less than eight new stations. The new service started on 3 October 1988 and was immediately so successful that Mid Glamorgan County Council applied to the Secretary of State for Wales for a £600,000 grant to purchase a Sprinter unit to provide an hourly service. The grant was blocked. BR itself came to the rescue and offered to provide an additional DMU, albeit a first-generation unit, to provide a better service. Even in South Wales, it is not all enlightenment since while Mid and South Glamorgan are positively pro-rail neighbouring Gwent turns its back on rail projects, preferring to invest in roads.

Indeed the overall score of the 1980s has been very uneven. For example, the early years of the decade saw numerous freight-only branches close

The 08.00 Blackpool North–Euston train passes Milton Keynes Central station at speed on 6 October 1984 powered by Class 87/0 No 87010 King Arthur.

131

because in most cases only a handful of wagonload traffic was being conveyed – uneconomically. The Lancashire branch to Rawtenstall closed on 4 December 1980, with the Wallingford branch from Cholsey following on 31 May 1981. The same month saw the end of the Brechin line while in 1982 the Forfar service ceased in June. A major closure took place on 27 November 1982 when the GN&GE Joint line closed between March and Spalding, together with the avoiding lines at Sleaford and Lincoln. Residual traffic was routed via Peterborough and this closure reflected the vastly changing freight scene as vacuum-braked freights gave way to air-braked company or block trains, precluding the necessity to marshal en route. Much of the huge yard at Whitemoor, March, closed.

1983 witnessed the last rites on perhaps the most famous freight line in the country – to Consett. The cessation of the steel plants sealed the fate of the line on which herculean battles took place daily in the haulage of loads of iron ore imported at Tyne Dock up the ferocious gradients to Consett.

Another historical line saw its last BR train on 26 September 1983 when the Cornish Wenford Bridge line was officially closed, its latter role being entirely devoted to the china clay traffic.

Meanwhile, on the passenger front, the four-mile Sanderstead–Elmers End line witnessed funereal acts on 13 May 1983. Another Southern Region service

Hardly looking like a suburban station in the densely populated Croydon area of south London is Coombe Road which closed at the end of the 1982/3 timetable with the ending of services on the Elmers End–Sanderstead line. 2-Epb unit No 5723 halts at the station whilst working the 17.30 Elmers End to Sanderstead on 15 April 1983.

axed was that between Tunbridge Wells Central and Eridge which finished on 6 July 1985. One day earlier, the Stratford to Tottenham Hale service in the east end of London bade farewell to passengers.

One closure – the Clayton West branch service which ran from Huddersfield – finally succumbed on 22 January 1983, because the West Yorkshire PTA declined to provide the subsidy. A similar casualty was the Kilmacolm branch which ended on 8 January 1983, because the Strathclyde PTA would support it no longer. The irony is that within five years, investigations started with a view to relaying part of the canal route to Kilmacolm as far as Paisley for a new passenger service! Building on the trackbed precludes a new service from serving the whole of the former route.

1983 witnessed the opening on 16 May of the first stretch of new main line built for over half a century – the 23.5km Selby Diversion line, replacing the former main line via Selby which closed completely between York Chaloner's Whin Junction and Selby North Junction.

Since the introduction of the business sectors of BR, Railfreight has not been slow to totally eliminate certain freight-only routes where an alternative existed, albeit, invariably longer. The Walsall–Lichfield, Manchester South Loop line and the Skelton–Arpley lines are cases in point. With the drastic decline in the coalmining industry, numerous branches to mines have closed, some of them quite lengthy, such as the Cynheidre and Maerdy branches in South Wales. Two 1989 closures were the Oakamoor and Caldon Low branches in the Stoke area which yielded their sand and stone traffic to road competition.

However, even in the world of freight, revival is taking place. The Annbank–Mauchline line which closed in 1984 was never lifted but merely mothballed. This prudent act paid off, for it reopened in 1988 to provide a shorter route for the coal traffic from Knockshinnoch to Ayr. Likewise, the Mickle Trafford to Dee Marsh line reopened for business on 1 September 1986. It originally closed to freight traffic on 14 May 1984.

One worrying aspect concerning the reopening of freight lines to passengers is that invariably where such revivals have taken place, BR has badly underestimated the level of business. The line to Bathgate, reopened to passengers on 24 March 1986 (including two new stations at Uphall and Livingston) at a cost of £1.5million shared by six public bodies expected to see a top figure of 400,000 passengers annually. This figure was rapidly exceeded and by 1989 was carrying one million passengers annually, necessitating lengthening platforms at several stations along its route at a cost of £60,000.

Worthy of mention in this review of closures and revivals is the widely applauded reprieve by Chris Green, director of Network SouthEast, of London's Marylebone station on 30 April 1986. BR had proposed closure of this famous station, but the growth of the commuter traffic meant that London Underground would not be able to cope. This station and line is now the subject of a multi-million pound investment scheme. Mr Green was also behind the move to relay the track on the abandoned freight-only link

133

Cardiff Cathays. One of many new stations opened with the help of local government finance. This view, taken during the first month of operation, shows three-car unit No C312 entering the station working the 11.35 (Sundays) Treherbert to Barry service on 30 October 1983.

between Blackfriars and Faringdon, thereby linking the electric systems north and south of the Thames. The new 'Thameslink' service started in May, 1987 and presently carries 20,000 passengers daily.

One famous London station did close. We gave our regards to Broad Street on 27 June 1986 when the last train pulled out, the site required for redevelopment.

The 1980s cause célèbre was of course the battle of the Settle & Carlisle. If ever there was proof needed that public opinion works, this is it. This famous line's deliberate run-down, closure proposals (three in total), the unbelievable fight by the public, culminating in 35,000 objectors during the five-year fight, was an object lesson to BR and the government. It was the latter who, unable to find a private buyer, announced on 11 April 1989 that BR must continue to operate the 72 mile route, a triumph for the three co-ordinating bodies – Transport 2000, The Settle & Carlisle Action Committee and the Friends of the Settle & Carlisle. This mammoth battle vividly demonstrated how inextricably railways are tied to politics. The reprieve of the S&C, besides marking the rightful conclusion to a tale of deceit and neglect, was also the first closure proposal vetoed by the Conservative Government under Mrs Thatcher.

The ever-changing railway saw several large marshalling yards close. Severn Tunnel yard went in October 1987, and Margam Hump yard closed on 31 October 1988, being replaced by the new 18 road Knuckle yard to cater for the huge growth in steel business, most of which travels in block trains. It was the same story which brought about the downfall of another huge yard – Tyne – in October 1989. The virtual cessation of the local trip workings, coupled with the growth in company trains (affecting the payloads of Speedlink services) meant that the reduction of actual Speedlink services could not justify the retention of a separate yard at Tyne (opened in 1961) – much of which handled Railfreight's Metals sub-sector business. Thus the healthy growth of a particular commodity – in this case steel – actually caused a closure.

The passenger scenario is more interesting. There seems to be no let-up with the continuing rise in patronage, even in the Network SouthEast area where the August 1989 approval to spend £257million on Networker units will inevitably attract more passengers when they are introduced.

On the passenger side, interest in the 1990s will centre on Provincial's split between the highly successful Sprinter Express routes and the also-rans. How do you privatise a business of numerous loss-makers? With the road-orientated Department of Transport constantly pressurising British Rail to examine all its options on loss-making services, the spectre of 'bustitution' is never far away. A test case was the proposed closure of the Gainsborough Central–Wrawby Junction, Barnetby, section of line used by Sheffield–Cleethorpes trains.

The separate announcement by BR in 1989 that it was proposing closure of the Doncaster–Gainsborough line was a surprise for there are many lines which lose more money than this with its nine daily trains. No sooner

Deltic No 55003 Meld leaves the now closed and lifted section of the East Coast main line via Selby at Chaloners Whin Junction while working the 14.05 King's Cross–York on 18 May 1980. The diversion opened in 1983.

The line between Eridge and Tunbridge Wells Central closed in July 1985. Here a month before closure Class 207 demu No 1306 leaves Eridge with the 14.35 from Uckfield to Victoria, to be followed by unit No 1310 (in platform 1 on the right) forming the 14.59 to Tonbridge via Tunbridge Wells.

had the announcement been made than it was withdrawn, pending deliberations by Lincolnshire County Council as to whether subsidisation could be considered as a way of continuance. Some sceptics have been quick to see that this could well be a familiar pointer to the future – suggest a service for closure in the hope that the relevant council will come up with the money to reprieve it. This transfers the onus from government subsidy to the local people who, should the council refuse, will themselves be 'blamed' for the service closure.

In total one can only marvel at the numerous stations opened in the 1980s and it is pleasing to note that many more are in the pipeline. The growth of BR stations in recent years is heartwarming for pro-rail supporters and the figures speak for themselves, 1986 = 2,526, 1987 = 2,530, 1988 = 2,554, 1989 = 2,561. A list of specific openings follows. Some ironically have been brought about by road congestion caused by the railway's erstwhile competitor, the private car. Many of the reopenings were under the 'Speller' rule: Tony Speller's 1981 Bill made it possible for services to reopen experimentally without the need to go through the formal closure procedures in the event of failure. Some were the direct result of campaigning by the Railway Development Society and the list is almost a tribute to it. It should be added that though this book is about BR, the 1980s also saw the opening of the last section of the Tyne & Wear Metro in March 1984 and the launch of the still-expanding Docklands Light Railway in July 1987. Both produced passenger levels far greater than forecast and have encouraged more planning of urban light railways.

136

BR in the 1980s
Openings (some reopenings on old or new sites)

17.3.80	Bury Interchange	24.3.86	Livingston North
12.5.80	Hackney Central	24.3.86	Uphall
12.5.80	Hackney Wick	10.5.86	South Wigston
12.5.80	Moulsecoomb	12.5.86	Cwmbran
6.10.80	Birchwood	12.5.86	Langley Mill
5.1.81	Dronfield	12.5.86	Telford Central
22.5.81	Honeybourne	12.5.86	Tiverton Parkway
24.6.81	New Holland	12.5.86	Winnersh Triangle
5.10.81	Kentish Town West	25.5.86	Polegate
5.10.81	Wetheral	14.6.86	Meadowbank
1.3.82	Fitzwilliam	7.7.86	Godley
15.3.82	Valley	14.7.86	Armathwaite
22.3.82	Blaenau Ffestiniog	14.7.86	Dent
26.4.82	Deighton	14.7.86	Garsdale
17.5.82	Crossflatts	14.7.86	Horton in Ribblesdale
17.5.82	Milton Keynes Central	14.7.86	Kirkby Stephen
17.5.82	Watton-at-Stone	14.7.86	Langwathby
2.8.82	Chapeltown	14.7.86	Lazonby
4.12.82	Vicarage Road	14.7.86	Ribblehead
13.12.82	Slaithwaite	15.9.86	Ardrossan Harbour
16.5.83	Pinhoe	29.9.86	Hall i'th Wood
16.5.83	Sandwell & Dudley	29.9.86	London Fields
17.5.83	Dalston Kingsland	29.9.86	Welham Green
12.9.83	Bramley	29.9.86	Ynyswen
3.10.83	Cathays	29.9.86	Ystrad Rhondda
3.10.83	Runcorn East	29.9.86	Burnley Manchester Road
3.10.83	Templecombe	24.11.86	Eastbrook
21.11.83	Moss Side	19.1.87	Ardrossan Town
9.1.84	Bache	8.3.87	Bolton Trinity Street
10.4.84	Saltaire	13.4.87	Blackpool Pleasure Beach
12.5.84	Kilmaurs	13.4.87	Corby
12.5.84	Auchinleck	29.4.87	Ty Glas
14.5.84	Bedford St Johns	1.5.87	East Garforth
14.5.84	Lostock Hall	9.5.87	Bicester Town
9.7.84	Sherburn in Elmet	11.5.87	Hag Fold
23.7.84	South Bank	11.5.87	Heysham Harbour
3.9.84	Melton	11.5.87	Lake
15.9.84	Dyce	11.5.87	Rotherham Central
1.10.84	Dunston	11.5.87	Salford Crescent
6.10.84	Livingston South	11.5.87	Wester Hailes
15.10.84	Humphrey Park	27.6.87	Conwy
26.11.84	Silkstone Common	30.6.87	Coalbrookdale
17.3.85	Eltham	5.7.87	Chee Dale Halt
23.3.85	Mills Hill	3.8.87	Coatbridge Central
1.5.85	Loch Awe	3.8.87	Gateshead Metro Centre
6.5.85	Loch Eil Outward Bound	7.9.87	Frizinghall
9.5.85	South Gyle	28.9.87	Moor Street
13.5.85	Bridge of Allan	3.10.87	Haddenham & Thame
13.5.85	Flowery Field		Parkway
13.5.85	Homerton	5.10.87	Danescourt
13.5.85	Melksham	5.10.87	Fairwater
13.5.85	Longbeck	5.10.87	Ninian Park
17.5.85	Portleven	5.10.87	Curriehill
20.5.85	Roughton Road	5.10.87	Snow Hill
30.6.85	Dunrobin	2.11.87	Waun-Gron Park
18.8.85	Smithy Bridge	30.11.87	Sandal & Agbrigg
30.9.85	Bromborough Rake	21.4.88	Cononley
30.9.85	Derker	24.4.88	Balloch
4.11.85	Lisvane & Thornhill	25.4.88	Cottingley
4.11.85	Ryder Brow	14.5.88	Bedworth
24.3.86	Bathgate	16.5.88	Goldthorpe

The new town development of Telford in Shropshire saw the opening of Telford Central station located on the Wolverhampton to Shrewsbury line on 12 May 1986. Class 47/4 No 47432 arrives on the first day of operation with the 13.33 Shrewsbury to Euston train.

16.5.88	Halewood
16.5.88	Lostock Junction
16.5.88	Thurnscoe
16.5.88	Newbury Racecourse
22.5.88	Stanhope
20.6.88	Falls of Cruachan
12.7.88	Outwood
16.8.88	Overpool
1.10.88	Arlesey
3.10.88	Musselburgh
3.10.88	Martins Heron
3.10.88	Aberycynon North
3.10.88	Aberdare
3.10.88	Cwmbach
3.10.88	Fernhill
3.10.88	Mountain Ash
3.10.88	Penrhiwceiber
22.10.88	How Wood

28.11.88	Lichfield Trent Valley High Level
28.11.88	Burley Park
3.4.89	Tutbury & Hatton
8.4.89	Hednesford
8.4.89	Cannock
8.4.89	Landywood
17.4.89	Bloxwich
15.5.89	Airbles
15.5.89	Greenfaulds
15.5.89	Islip
15.5.89	Milliken Park
15.5.89	Stepps
15.5.89	Berry Brow
15.5.89	Yate
15.5.89	Dodsworth
15.5.89	Drumgelloch

Closures

3.5.80	Llantarnam Junction–Furnace Sidings, Blaenavon
14.2.81	Rawtenstall branch (from Bury)
2.5.81	Brechin branch (including Kinnaber Junction)
30.5.81	South Shields branch (later reopened for Metro operation)
31.5.81	Wallingford branch (from Cholsey)
18.7.81	Woodhead route (Penistone to Hadfield)
18.7.81	Worsborough branch (Penistone to Wath)
5.6.82	Forfar branch (from Stanley Junction)
Oct. 82	Newcastle–Blaydon via Scotswood Bridge
6.11.82	Torrington branch (from Barnstaple)
27.11.82	Spalding–March (Joint line)
27.11.82	Lincoln and Sleaford avoiding lines
8.1.83	Kilmacolm branch
22.1.83	Clayton West branch (from Shepley)
13.5.83	Sanderstead–Elmers End
26.9.83	Wenford Bridge branch (from Bodmin Road)
30.9.83	Coulsdon North station
6.2.84	Radipole station
17.2.84	Consett branch (from Ouston Junction)
19.3.84	Lichfield–Walsall
12.5.84	Bedford St Johns station
4.6.84	Cudworth–Stairfoot Junction

24.9.83	York, Chaloners Whin Junction–Selby, Barlby North Junction
1.10.84	Normanton, Goose Hill Junction–Wath Road Junction
4.3.85	Eltham Park station
11.5.85	Lincoln St Marks station
11.5.85	New Hadley station
5.7.85	Stratford–Tottenham Hale
6.7.85	Tunbridge Wells–Eridge
8.7.85	Warrington Arpley–Skelton Junction
11.10.85	Rose Heyworth branch
27.6.86	Broad Street station
22.8.86	Maerdy branch
26.9.86	Cefn Onn station
28.9.86	Balloch Pier
16.4.87	Bottesford West–Newark Northgate
8.5.87	Royton station
26.9.87	Birmingham Moor Street old terminus
8.7.88	Rowntree Halt
30.8.88	Oakamoor branch
2.10.88	Rotherham Masborough station
20.1.89	Burton Lane Jct, York–Layerthorpe
20.1.89	East Dereham–North Elmham
7.2.89	Caldon Low branch (from Leek Brook Junction)
15.6.89	Elswick branch (from Newcastle Central)
25.8.89	Carbis Wharf branch (from Bugle)
22.12.89	Chinnor branch (from Princes Risborough)

Broad Street station on 18 July 1983. Class 501 emus (now all withdrawn) form the 11.35 and 11.54 trains for Richmond. Today Broad Street is just a memory. North London line trains were diverted into Liverpool Street via a new connection.

12
A REVOLUTION
IN MOTIVE POWER

BR's motive-power policy was rapidly turned on its head with the abandonment of two sacred principles: sectorisation saw the end of the common-user policy for locomotives and passenger multiple units: and no longer was it accepted that life-expired main-line cast-offs should spend their last days propping up secondary services.

The locomotive fleet may have become slimmer and generally older, but it still ended the decade in better overall shape thanks to this revised policy; new maintenance procedures, and heavy expenditure on refurbishment of key types, also helped. The multiple-unit fleet was transformed virtually beyond recognition. It was goodbye to the last vestiges of pre-war LMS and LNER designs, and even the slam-door concept that the Southern Railway bequeathed to its nationalised successor was displaced from many important commuter routes.

To the enthusiast, the loss of no less than fourteen locomotive designs was countered by the application of highly distinctive sector liveries, all the more interesting because of the number of attempts made before the final choices were made. The apparent 'if it moves, renumber it' policy was also a major source of interest.

InterCity saw its future in push-pull electric traction, modernised High Speed Trains on non-electrified routes, and only a handful of diesel-locomotive-hauled services on feeder and cross-country routes.

Provincial resisted InterCity's relatively modern but redundant 1960s coaching stock, and nailed its colours firmly to the mast of the Sprinter DMU. The two-car diesel unit provided ultimate flexibility and low operating costs, plus the chance to attract new business with smart new stock operating on faster schedules. The government accepted the argument, and approved the investment.

Network SouthEast, struggling to cope with its massive upsurge in business, proceeded with complete refurbishment of serviceable 1960s stock and started massive investment in new trains, notably its Networker.

Parcels was happy to operate with a small fleet of locomotives and hauled stock, plus a fleet of 1950s passenger DMUs converted for load carrying.

Railfreight is now by far the biggest user of locomotives. The restructure of the coal, aggregates, Speedlink, petroleum and metals businesses made it relatively easy to identify and organise separate sub-sector fleets, increasingly recognised by the new grey livery decorated with esoteric fleet symbols and depot badges.

140

Finally, the departmental, engineering side also laid claim to its own clearly defined fleet of engines, which could be profitably loaned to the sectors at times of peak demand.

New Classes. New locomotive classes of the eighties were just five, all high-power main liners. After nearly thirty years, the first AC electric Co-Co locomotive arrived in 1986 in the shape of the prototype 5,850hp, 125mph Class 89, built under contract by BREL Crewe with electrical gear by Brush Traction. After trials, it pioneered locomotive-hauled electric trains over the northern extension of East Coast main line electrification to Peterborough in 1988.

The Class 89 was notable for its lack of teething troubles, sadly not experienced by the two other new electric designs. The first BREL/GEC Class 90, an updated version of the Class 87 Bo-Bo, emerged from Crewe in mid-1988, but it was many months before the state of the art electronics were mastered. Delivery of the final members of the class was still taking place at the end of the decade, but the early members had by then settled into their routine of West Coast InterCity push-pull passenger duties with similar-looking new driving van trailers at the opposite end, plus freights from the North to the East Coast ports via the newly electrified North London link.

The 09.20 for Liverpool Lime Street leaves Euston on 10 July 1989 powered by Class 90 No 90009 Royal Show. On the left, Class 87/0 No 87010 King Arthur awaits departure time with the 09.45 to Carlisle. It is interesting to note that bullhead rail is still in evidence some forty years after the infant British Railways adopted flat-bottom rail as standard.

141

However, the new build highlight of the 1980s was undoubtedly the 6,000hp-plus, 140mph Class 91 intended for the full King's Cross–Leeds/ Edinburgh electrification in 1991. GEC supplied the equipment for assembly at BREL Crewe, and although software problems delayed entry into service until the early part of 1989, the prototype batch of ten (another twenty-one are on order) were a regular sight on King's Cross–Peterborough commuter and some Leeds service by the end of the year. The traction combination with an HST power car converted to a driving trailer and only seven HST coaches made mincemeat of conventional timings.

The heavy freight diesel replacement policy was a muddle from beginning to end. First, BR curtailed the production line of the obsolete over-complicated Class 56 Co-Cos in 1984 when the 135th example emerged from BREL Crewe. This overlapped the appearance of the first modular construction Class 58 from Doncaster, mechanically similar but theoretically cheaper to maintain. This so-called new standard machine found itself overtaken by new technology and failed to attract hoped-for export orders, only running to fifty examples. Although they were all allocated to coal traffic in the East Midlands, their arrival coincided with the miners' strike, and in truth BR only tolerated the construction of so many because the components were already on order.

General Motors of America believed they had made a major breakthrough into the British market in 1985 when they persuaded Foster Yeoman to buy four specially constructed 3,300hp locomotives to haul heavy stone traffic

Propelling the 10.10 Leeds–King's Cross InterCity service, Class 91 No 91007 passes under the Wood Green flyover on the approaches to Alexandra Park station on 23 September 1989.

from their Merehead quarry to locations in the South East. Rules were relaxed to allow the first privately owned locomotives unlimited access to the national rail network.

By now urgently needing at least 100 replacements for its geriatric locomotive fleet, Railfreight initially appeared to show deep interest in its own General Motors stud, but in the event the order went to Brush Traction of Loughborough. The arrival of the first Class 60 Co-Cos in the autumn of 1989 would spell the wholesale demise of many thirty-year-old Class 20s, 31s, 33s and 47s.

Farewell. Fourteen locomotive types were eliminated during the 1980s, although examples of all but five have been secured for preservation. The most sadly missed type is undoubtedly the twenty-two English Electric Class 55 Deltics from the East Coast main line. Their last runs at the end of 1981 were witnessed by scenes not seen since the end of steam when literally thousands either embarked on farewell trips or crowded platform ends for a last glimpse of the 3,300hp machines that were as popular as the LNER Gresley steam Pacifics they replaced. Displaced by High Speed Trains, much of their final year was remarkably spent on new territory including York–Liverpool runs. No less than six survive in preservation.

Almost equal euphoria was attracted by the English Electric Class 40s, the first large-volume design introduced after the 1955 Modernisation Plan. Underpowered, overweight and outdated, the once 200 strong fleet, affectionately known as 'Whistlers' was in decline from the mid-1970s, and when major overhauls ceased at BREL Crewe in 1981 it was only a question of time before they disappeared first from top link Eastern Region duties, and finally in 1985 freight workings originating from the North West.

BR's own acknowledgement of the Class 40s' popularity, and therefore revenue potential, was the renovation of the 1958 pioneer locomotive D200 to working order, and original livery, for use on special trains for a full three years after the rest of the class had been retired. It is now in the National Railway Museum, and another five were purchased privately.

Less fuss was created by the no less significant demise of two important products from the Derby Locomotive Works. The 'Peaks' once numbered 193 of three similar types with twelve-cylinder Sulzer power units in heavy bodyshell on four-axle plate-frame bogies. Withdrawal of the prototype Class 44 series of ten was completed in 1981, and a start was then made on the production Class 45 and 46 fleets. Displaced first from the North East/South West corridor and East Coast services, they had largely disappeared from their traditional Midland main line haunts by the mid-1980s, and the arrival of Class 156 Sprinter DMUs displaced the last survivors from Trans-Pennine workings in the summer of 1988. Although a handful have been preserved, BR's attempt to emulate the success of the D200 project was short-lived when the selected example suffered a terminal breakdown.

It is hard to imagine that there were once almost 600 Sulzer-engined Bo-Bo locomotives in the 1,160–1,250hp range, because a mere thirty-two survived at the end of 1989. The entire BR fleet of Classes 24 and 25 had gone by the beginning of 1978. The Birmingham RC&W-built Class 27s disappeared soon afterwards (despite expensive overhauls only months before), leaving only the 1958/9 Birmingham-built Class 26 surviving on specialist duties in Southern Scotland.

The closure of the Manchester–Sheffield/Wath 1,500V DC freight route via Woodhead tunnel in 1982 spelt the inevitable end of the LNER-design Class 76 Bo-Bos, which although far from life-expired could not work anywhere else. The London Midland Region also gave up with its older AC electric locomotives, first its troublesome contractor-built Classes 82, 83 and 84, and then with new designs coming along, Classes 81 and 85 were into their last days.

Almost unnoticed was the exit of the last 0-4-0 locomotive, latterly represented by the 204hp Andrew Barclay Class 06 dock shunter in Scotland (and departmental service in England), and the three curious Class 13 700hp hump shunters formed of two Class 08s in permanent formations.

Modifications. Large-scale modifications were made to the BR locomotive fleet to both keep them running, and create a stop-gap before the arrival of new motive power for both passenger and freight use.

Two long-running conversion programmes reached their conclusion at last. Barring a handful for specialist duties, every locomotive was equipped with air brakes. This involved a massive conversion programme on Classes 08, 20, 26, 27, 31 and 37, often outside normal overhaul schedules. Steam-heated hauled stock was also eradicated, and the response was the reclassification of more Class 31/4s and 47/4s, plus the first Class 37/4s.

Longer-term planning forced BR to embark upon life-extension programmes for several locomotive types expected to be needed until well into the 1990s, although they were halted in 1989 before being completed.

English Electric Class 37s in particular were subjected to near-total rebuilds, involving replacement of the main generator with an alternator, regeared CP7 bogies, and in some cases Ruston or Mirrlees power unit, electric-heat generator, or ballast weights added to provide extra adhesion for particular freight work. Thus, one standard locomotive design evolved into six specialist types.

Many Brush-built Class 31s were equipped with ETH generators and given a major body overhaul, while some Class 47s were similarly treated. The Class 50 refurbishment programme was completed, although they are destined for a short life, while limited work was also carried out on Class 20s, 26s and 33s to see them through to the arrival of new designs.

On reflection, costly mistakes were made with both the Class 27s and 45s, whose short careers could not possibly have justified the lavish life-extension work carried out on them.

High Speed Trains. The eight-year High Speed Train power car production line came to an end at BREL Crewe works in August 1982 with the delivery

Romanian-built Brush Class 56 No 56015 at Coalville on 11 June 1989. It carries Railfreight coal sub-sector livery and is allocated to Toton (TO) depot.

of the 198th and final example, although strengthening of the fixed coach rakes meant the final augmentation trailer did not appear until the spring of 1985. Healthy business, and integration of the Midland main line into the HST network, saw most of the fixed rakes expanded to eight vehicles.

Opponents of the two locomotives for each train concept were vindicated by a series of stress defects and overheating of the Paxman Valenta 2,250hp power units, and it was agreed to re-engine four Western Region examples with Mirrlees units. (It is the long-term plan to re-engine 140 more.)

Trailer-wise, complaints from guards about excessive noise in the guard's compartment at the rear of the power car saw an order for 101 second-class trailers hurriedly modified to include a small compartment for them.

Pullman units were created for prestige services to Newcastle, Leeds, Sheffield, Cardiff and the West of England, while most other trailer kitchen firsts (TKFs) were converted to hauled stock. The original concept of separate kitchen/restaurants and buffets for HSTs was too ambitious given shorter journey times and changing eating habits.

Mid-life refurbishment with new first- and second-class seating has justifiably continued the HST's popularity. Externally, the repainting from blue and grey to the new InterCity house style was practically complete as

145

The bodyshells of Class 60 Nos 60005 and 60006 under construction inside the Procor Works at Horbury on 25 April 1989.

1989 drew to a close. As for embellishments, the people organising naming ceremonies seemed to be outnumbered by other policymakers whose desire was to see them progressively removed. No one was really sure why.

Diesel Units. The Sprinter DMU was one of BR's greatest success stories of the 1980s – though there were severe setbacks from late deliveries, unreliability of one design, and a near-disastrous flirtation with cheap-to-build railbuses.

The decision to press ahead with new builds on a large scale was based on Provincial's conviction that it could reduce its losses if given the freedom to operate cost-effective diesel-mechanical rolling stock, allowing shorter but more frequent trains, than having to take on InterCity's weary cast-off locos and hauled stock. Added to that was the desire to eradicate all vehicles with asbestos insulation by 1988, a target not in fact achieved.

The truism that you get what you pay for was ably demonstrated by the decision in 1981 to replace ageing first-generation DMU fleets on non-

Class 60 No 60002
Capability Brown
*undergoes trials at Derby
RTC on 9 October 1989.*

electrified outer suburban lines and remote branches with low-cost bus-type bodies on four-wheeled underframes. The prototype Leyland two-car Class 140 unit appeared in 1981, and other fleets quickly appeared from Leyland, BREL and Andrew Barclay as Classes 141, 142, 143 and 144. By 1987, the honeymoon was over. Large numbers were laid up with a multiplicity of gearbox, transmission, body and wheelset problems. Old-generation units were patched up even further beyond their expected life span. In one curious case, Cornish services inherited the units delivered there thirty years previously!

The Sprinter DMUs, conventionally engineered units built by BREL, Leyland and Metro-Cammell, Classes 150, 151, 154, 155, 156 and 158, were considerably more successful and by the end of the decade in charge of the mainstay of Provincial services literally from Wick to Penzance. Although the first units were somewhat spartan, the later builds were well equipped and responsible for a sizeable upturn in passenger business on some routes. Again, there was a slight hiccup when the entire Leyland Class 155 fleet were

147

withdrawn for almost a year with door troubles; they opened while the train was running!

It was goodbye therefore, albeit slower than planned, to large numbers of vintage units. The asbestos-contaminated Cravens Class 105s, Gloucester Class 100s and Park Royal Class 103s were completely wiped out, while the advancing army of Sprinters began to make heavy inroads into the enormous numbers of Metro-Cammell and BR-built units.

The Southern Region's small domestic fleet of diesel-electric units was trimmed back thanks to the completion of the Tonbridge–Hastings and East Grinstead electrification. By the end of the decade, new electrification projects meant the writing was on the wall for the surviving English Electric-engined Class 205 and 207 units.

AC Electric Units. Commuting became fashionable again in the 1980s, and BR responded with new suburban electrification schemes, over a thousand new electric passenger vehicles and (when replacement finance was not available) 1950s units given the asbestos-removal treatment and a mid-life facelift.

By contrast to the erratic and often wasteful locomotive policy, BR seemed determined to extract maximum mileage out of its EMU fleet, sometimes moving entire fleets from one line to another. Standardisation has reached such a level that there are now only five main types of AC unit, the pre-1960 Southern Region-inspired slam-door units (Classes 302–8), express (Class

At the close of the decade there were only two examples of the Class 03 diesel mechanical shunter remaining in stock, both on the Isle of Wight. Here No 03073 (since withdrawn) stands at Duke Street in Birkenhead Docks on 23 August 1988.

309), modern slam-door (Classes 310/312), Scotland/Manchester suburban sliding door (Classes 303/311), inner suburban sliding door (Classes 313–315), and modern outer-suburban based on the Mark 3 coach bodyshell (Classes 317–21). Only one class of AC unit, the pre-war design LNER Class 306 disappeared completely.

Network SouthEast provided its four showpiece routes north of London with new rolling stock, Bedford–St Pancras, King's Cross–Cambridge/Peterborough, Liverpool Street–Cambridge, and Euston–Northampton. First was the newly energised Bedford–St Pancras route which was the first home of forty-eight four-car Class 317s. They entered traffic in 1982 after a series of teething troubles, and union resistance to one-man operation.

Their stay was brief however. The integration of the Bed-Pan service with Thameslink operation from 1988 onwards, allowed dual voltage use of the similar, brand-new Class 319 units, dispatch of the 317s to the Great Northern and London Midland, and closure of the recently modernised Cricklewood maintenance depot into the bargain.

King's Cross–Cambridge/Peterborough outer suburban services, a bodged combination of electric units to Hitchin and Royston, and DMUs and HSTs over the non-electric gap, was brought together at the end of the decade, courtesy of two collections of four-car 317s, a purpose-built second batch of twenty-five units, and thirteen of the earlier series. Class 313s continued to look after the inner suburban system, and the now non-standard 1977-series Class 312s were packed off to the Colchester line. As GN business continued to grow, the solution was simply to obtain more slightly soiled Class 317s from somewhere or other.

Cambridge-line passengers, celebrating the establishment of an electric link to Bishop's Stortford and Liverpool Street, felt short-changed when the only trains BR could offer were facelifted 1960 built Class 305 slam-door stock, actually older than the hauled stock it replaced. After a brief spell with ex-GN Class 312s, relief came in 1988 with brand-new Class 321s, sporting a smart exterior, but in truth little more than a Class 319 Thameslink unit without the end gangway connection.

Apart from seeing the replacement of LNER-design inner-suburban Class 306s, Colchester, Southend, Bishop's Stortford, Hertford and Chingford-line travellers will have to wait until the 1990s for their new stock. In the meantime, most of the original Classes 302, 304, 305, 307, 308 have been turned into open saloons and given new seating and gangways. The gap left by the withdrawal of the worst examples has been filled with Class 312s, and ex-London Midland 310s.

Now almost thirty years old, and arguably BR's best-ever buys, the Mark 1 based Class 309 'Clacton' units, continued their relentless treks across the Essex countryside, now with new seating, a new livery, and with the extension of wires to Ipswich and Norwich, the chance to break out of their traditional operational straitjacket.

Euston–Northampton services, now recognised in their own right, jumped the queue in 1989 to receive new Class 321s with first-class facility. It also

(Opposite above) Given a new lease of life. Rebuilt English Electric Class 37 No 37272, now ETH fitted Class 37/4 No 37431 Sir Powys/County of Powys *stands at Cardiff with the 09.50 Swansea to Portsmouth train, 16 February 1988. The Cardiff Canton-based locomotive was modified in 1986.*

(Opposite below) The first of the Class 47s – or Brush Type 4s as they were known when D1500 appeared in 1962 – still hard at work from Gateshead depot in 1987. Here No 47401, as it is now numbered and carrying the name North Eastern *which it both received and lost during the 1980s, nears Greenfield on a Trans-Pennine service, the 17.03 Liverpool to Newcastle on 19 June 1987. The train is made up of Mk2A and C stock in Provincial 'Trans-Pennine' colours with a Mk1 full brake in blue and grey at the rear.*

Class 26/0 No 26005, in old Railfreight grey, stands at Eastfield depot on 12 June 1988. At the end of the decade all the remaining members of the class were based here.

HST. Nos 43119+43065 emerging from Calton Hill Tunnel at the start of the journey with the 09.35 Edinburgh–King's Cross service on Sunday 21 June 1987. The leading power car is in the older Inter-City livery and has its number rather than a set number displayed on the front end. This reflects a change in attitude, the power cars are now seen as separate locomotive units. The visible Mk3 trailers are still in blue and grey.

became clear that the 319/321 design would be built for some time yet.

Scotland's only new acquisitions during the decade were twenty-one Class 318s, three-car versions of the Class 317, to service the newly electrified Glasgow–Ayr/Largs routes, although 1989 also witnessed the first withdrawals proper (apart from accident victims or asbestos units) of the original Pressed Steel 1959 'Blue Train' Class 303s, whose unrefurbished examples are due for early replacement by 100mph Class 321-type Class 320s.

Greater Manchester, unable to finance its own units, was content to take up twelve redundant ex-Scottish Class 303s, at the same time reducing its fleet of equally geriatric slam-door Class 304s from four to three cars.

DC electric units. Apart from an influx of long-awaited sliding-door stock for inner suburban units and a small batch of unpopular Weymouth–Waterloo stocks, the headlines for the Southern Region's vast DC electric fleet were disappointingly dull. It was a long tale of low-cost facelifts, make do and mend, and cover up the cracks in a coat of Network SouthEast red, white and blue paint.

This was no more evident than on the Isle of Wight at the end of 1989, which seemed to be going backwards despite getting new stock. The replacement units, renovated life-expired 1938 ex-Underground vehicles, were fifty-one years old to begin with. It replaced 1923 stock, which was incidentally only forty-four years old at the time it was moved to the island!

South London commuters who have travelled practically all their working lives on dreary Bulleid-influenced 4-SUB and EPB units would have celebrated the arrival from York in 1981 of the first Class 455 four-car units, which, in three batches, eventually ran to 137.

Elsewhere, it was very much the same. Eastleigh and Horwich shared a rebuilding programme for ninety-seven four-car units of 1951 EPB stock, and two-car units followed before the scheme was halted in the face of more orders for new stock. Kent Coast travellers saw their Mark 1 based Class 411 4-CEPS taken to BREL Swindon (the last major coach contract before the works closed) for a thorough facelift that also included new windows and double glazing. The similar Class 421 4-CIGS, and unpopular Class 423 4-VEPS were also processed, but at lower cost.

Apart from the 4-SUBS, traffic levels meant there was little chance for stock to fall out of the bottom of the cascade. This was reserved for those with asbestos, including most of the two-car express-geared but still unpleasantly cramped 4-HAPS.

The extension of electrification from Bournemouth to Weymouth, completed in 1988, saw the arrival of the new streamlined 100mph Class 442, five-car buffet units with power-operated sliding doors, air conditioning, and the return of compartments for first-class travellers. The traditional Southern waste not, want not policy was perpetuated in the reuse of traction equipment from the Class 432 4-REPS they replaced.

InterCity's dedicated Victoria–Gatwick Express push-pull service launched in 1984 made little difference to domestic services, employing ex-LMR Mark 2f coaches formed into trailer sets with a 1959-type 2-HAP driving trailer

Colourful is perhaps the polite way to describe this BRCW three-car dmu set P460 with No 51317 the leading car. It is painted in British Telecom yellow livery with blue lettering. The unit is seen here leaving Plymouth working a shuttle service to Laira depot open day on 7 September 1985.

Class 142 Pacer diesel multiple unit No 142073 passes the Midland Railway signalbox at Hellifield South Junction while working the 11.33 Leeds to Morecambe service on 2 April 1988. The signalbox controls the junction with the Blackburn line which diverges to the left of the picture. The station is now an unstaffed halt.

converted to a driving van at one end, and a Class 73 locomotive at the other.

More thorough stock control completed the changed Southern scene as virtually all EMU units were renumbered to allow the first two digits to match their fleet status.

The London Midland Region, the only operator of wholly DC units, cut its varieties to just three. Conversion of the Manchester–Hadfield stub of the old Woodhead route from 1,500V DC operation to standard 25kV kissed goodbye to the eight 1954 Class 506s, ninety-two of which were used on Great Eastern services until 1982. LMS influence disappeared from Merseyside's Southport and Wirral electric routes with the demise of the pre-war three-car sliding-door stock of Classes 502 and 503. In their place came standard aluminium-bodied BR units, Class 507s brand new, and Class 508s second hand from the Southern. In decline almost since they were built, the North London line's BR-design Class 501s peacefully passed into oblivion, replaced by Class 313 dual-voltage units borrowed from the Great Northern.

So, very little pre-nationalisation influence is left on our increasingly standardised system. For the enthusiast there are two tiny pockets worth exploring however . . . London's Waterloo & City tube line, where the 1940 vintage cars sport NSE livery on the outside and Southern Railway ventilator grilles on the inside, and the individualistic Manchester–Bury line, where Lancashire & Yorkshire influence still shines through with battered 1959 BR stock rattling up and down the short, but unique 1,200V DC side contact third rail complete with semaphore signals. But not for much longer.

The first Class 158 Provincial Express vehicle, No 158701, is unveiled at Derby Railway Technical Centre on 9 October 1989.

New classes built during the 1980s

Locomotives

Type	No series	Builder	Date		Power	Total
Class 43	43002–198	BREL	1975–82	Bo-Bo	2250	196
Class 56	56001–135	Brush/BREL	1976–84	Co-Co	3250	135
Class 58	58001–50	BREL	1983–87	Co-Co	3300	50
Class 59	59001–5	Gen Mot USA	1985–89	Co-Co	3300	5
Class 60	60001–100	Brush	1989–	Co-Co	3100	100*
Class 89	89001	Brush/BREL	1987	Co-Co	5850	1
Class 90	90001–50	GEC/BREL	1987–	Bo-Bo	5000	50*
Class 91	91001–31	GEC/BREL	1988–	Bo-Bo	6100	31*

* Not all delivered

Diesel Multiple Units

Type	No series	Builder	Date	Cars	Total
Class 141	55502–40	Leyland/BREL	1984	2	20
Class 142	55542–792	Leyland/BREL	1985–86	2	96
Class 143	55642–91	Alexander/Barclay	1985–86	2	25
Class 144	55801–59	Alexander/BREL	1986–88	2/3	23
Class 150	55200–401	BREL	1984	3	6
	52101–7150	BREL	1985–86	2/3	136
	52201–7285		1986–87	2/3	170
Class 151	55202–403	Met-Cammell	1985	3	6
Class 155	52301–7347	Leyland	1987–88	2	84
Class 156	52401–7514	Met-Cammell	1988–89	2	228
Class 158	52701–8713	BREL	1989–	2/3	229*

Electric Multiple Units

Class 314	314201–16	BREL	1979	3	48
Class 315	315801–61	BREL	1981–82	4	244
Class 317	317301–72	BREL	1981–87	4	288
Class 318	318250–70	BREL	1985–87	3	63
Class 319	319001–	BREL	1987–	4	180†
Class 321	321301–	BREL	1988–	4	†
Class 442	2401–24	BREL	1987–88	5	120
Class 455	5701–43	BREL	1977–85	4	129
	5801–74	BREL	1981–84	4	222
	5901–20	BREL	1985	4	80
Class 457	7001	BREL	1981–85	4	4
Class 488	8201–10	BREL	1984	2/3	20
	8301–19	BREL	1984	3	57
Class 489	9101–10	BREL	1983–84	1	10
Class 507	507001–33	BREL	1978–80	3	99
Class 508	508101–43	BREL	1979–80	3	129

† Orders still being placed

Classes extinct during the 1980s

Locomotives

Type	No series as at 1.1.80	Builder	Gone by
Class 01	01001	Barclay	1981
Class 05	05001	Hunslet	1981
Class 06	06002–8	Barclay	1981
Class 13	13001–3	BR/EE	1985
Class 24	24081	BR	1980
Class 25	25001–912	BR	1987
Class 27	27001–212	BRCW	1987
Class 40	40001–199	EE	1985
Class 44	44004–8	BR	1980
Class 45	45001–150	BR	1989
Class 46	46001–56	BR	1984
Class 55	55001–22	EE	1982
Class 76	76001–56	BR/MV	1981
Class 82	82001–8	BRCW/EE	1987
Class 83	83001–15	BP/MV	1987
Class 84	84002–10	NB/GEC	1983

Diesel Multiple Units

Type	No series	Builder	Gone by
Class 103	50395–56165	Park Royal	1982
Class 105	53359–56482	Cravens	1989
Class 123	52087–59827	BR	1984
Class 124	51951–59842	BR	1984
Class 126	50936–79470	BR	1982

Diesel Electric Multiple Units

Type	No series	Builder	Gone by
Class 201	1001–7	BR	1986
Class 202	202001	BR	1988
Class 204	204001–4	BR	1988
Class 206	206101	BR	1988

Electric Multiple Units

Type	No series	Builder	Gone by
Class 306	306001–92	BR	1981
Class 405	4277–754	BR	1983
Class 501	61135–75188	BR	1985
Class 502	28312–29897	LMS	1980
Class 503	28371–29846	MC/BRCW	1985
Class 506	59401–59606	BR	1984

Life extension

Dual braked: Classes 08, 20, 26, 27, 31, 37.
Refurbished: Classes 26, 27, 31, 37, 50, 303, 305, 307, 308, 309, 310, 411, 412, 415, 416, 421, 422, 423.

Preserved

Sold from BR: Classes 01, 03, 05, 06, 07 (Ruston 0-6-0), 08, 15 (BTH Bo-Bo), 20, 24, 25, 26, 27, 35 (Beyer Peacock B-B), 40, 44, 45, 47, 55, 105, 127 (BR DMU), 502, 503, 506.
Other types sold from private industry, but ex-BR: Classes 02 (Yorkshire Engine 0-4-0), 04 (Drewry 0-6-0), 10 (Blackstone 0-6-0), 11 (LMS 0-6-0), 12 (SR 0-6-0), 14 (BR 0-6-0), 17 (Clayton B-B), 77 (BR Co-Co from Holland), LMS 0-6-0 (from France), unclassified North British 0-4-0.

On delivery from BREL York to Ilford, new class 321 emu No 321334 is reflected in the waters of the River Ouse as it passes Offord Cluney, near Huntingdon, on 31 March 1989.

A panoramic view of Waterloo on 21 August 1989 with Class 442 Wessex Electric No 2424 leading No 2410 and forming the 17.15 Royal Wessex to Weymouth and Poole.

13
SIGNALLING, SAFETY AND CONTROL

The 1980s saw the resignalling of the West of England main line in stages between Westbury and Totnes. Large mechanical boxes at such places as Westbury, Taunton and Newton Abbot were demolished and many fine GWR-pattern signals disappeared. The illustrations on pages 8 and 59 show Newton Abbot and Taunton during resignalling. Extensive resignalling also took place on the Midland main line. The colour-light replacements for the Leicester North Box semaphores are already in place in this view taken on 21 June 1986 with a Nottingham–St Pancras HST service gliding by.

'DING' rang the block bell at the right hand end of the block shelf in the signalbox. The signalman, one of the three regulars in East box, knew from the tone that it was the down main instrument. He replied with one beat on the bell tapper to let the man at the Junction know that he was ready for the message. Four beats in quick succession came back – 'Is line clear for express passenger train'. The East box signalman knew that the previous train had passed some while ago, the down main signals were at danger and caution and the points from the down main to down relief were set for the straight-through run on the main. He replied with four beats, 'line clear for express passenger train' and turned the block indicator from 'line blocked' to 'line clear'. Normally he offered the train straight on to West box and was about to do so when the telephone bell gave a coded ring, two short rings, a pause, two more short rings. That was someone calling him. 'East box' he called into the phone. 'That'll be the London before the Leeds which is twenty down. Behind the Leeds will be the clay empties so you can give them a run,' said a voice which he recognised as that of the Junction man. 'OK Jack', and with that he called the attention of West box and went through the same procedure – a procedure which with detail variations had its origins more than 130 years ago, yet which on BR in the 1980s is still used on a few main lines and quite a number of cross-country routes where mechanical signalling survives.

BR in the 1980s portrays a scene of great contrasts in railway signalling for, at the opposite extreme, is the latest in communication technology, microprocessors, mainframe computers, 'chips', and radio. Look in at one of BR's latest signalling control centres – now called Integrated Electronic Control Centres (IECCs) – and all you will see is a desk with visual display units (VDUs) which show diagrams of the line, with controls of signals from what look like typewriter keyboards or a 'mouse' – a control device aimed at the screen to trigger a signalling sequence. Solid state switching and interlocking replace electro-mechanical relays which have been the reliable norm for around eighty years.

In between these extremes are successive generations of signalling equipment which served BR in the 1980s; miniature levers for power operation (the standard of the 1920s and 1930s and still being installed after World War II), one-control-switch panels (pioneered by the LNER in the 1930s and used in a number of installations after World War II until the late 1950s), and entrance-exit panels with route-setting buttons placed geographically along the track diagram (again developed for the LNER just at the end

160

of the 1930s and all the vogue right into the 1980s, the last major installation being commissioned in South West England in 1987). But whereas all these developments followed a logical path, each new technique building on what had gone before with proven reliability and fail-safe features, the step into the world of computers, microchips, data transmission by wire, optical fibres, or radio was a great leap into the unknown as far as railway signalling was concerned. So reliability and fail-safe had to be extensively tested in all sorts of conditions; it was in the 1980s that BR was satisfied that the new technology could in fact be accepted in line service (as distinct from trials in parallel with conventional equipment). So was launched the great transformation which will set the pattern for the 1990s and into the next century.

But in all this the vital word is communication, whether it be man to man, man to lever, or button, lever to signal or points, relay to relay, microchip to signal or signal to driver. Let us go back to our mechanical signalbox.

The block system, in which the line was divided into sections, a signalbox at each boundary, with its principle of 'not more than one train in a block section on one line at a time' for absolute block working, relied to a large extent on the discipline of signalmen with all the possibilities of human error which that entailed. Gradually 'add-ons' in the form of treadles or track circuits helped to provide over the last eighty years a small amount of automation; from the 1930s new locking features were fitted to block instruments and signal levers which combined with track circuits meant that signals could not be cleared unless the block instrument for the section ahead was clear, and that in its turn the block instrument could not be cleared unless the previous train had been proved to have passed out of the section and the signals placed at danger and caution behind it. But these features, known as Welwyn control, following their introduction after the 1935 Welwyn Garden City collision, even by the 1980s were not universal on lines retaining mechanical signalling. A few of these older signalling installations still rely on signalmen not making mistakes.

Move now to another section of line, perhaps not too far away from the mechanical box and the revolution is stunning. The first thing that a visitor to an integrated electronic control centre (IECC) will notice is that the environment is akin to an office: air conditioned, few windows, subdued lighting, wall-to-wall carpeting, desks, swivel armchairs, visual display units, what appear to be typewriter keyboards and print-out machines. In the new IECCs the signalmen, controllers, operators, call them what you will, often do not see trains for real but only as moving blobs of red light along a track diagram on the screen. Tea comes from the mess room, not from the traditional pot boiled on a solid-fuel stove. As for the control of trains this is the age of automation, sometimes with junctions set automatically, controlled from the train describer.

Trains are shown by a four-character alpha-numerical code unique to each one or to the route in the case of suburban services. The identity code is transmitted from the adjoining IECC or signalling centre automatically as the train approaches the boundary between the two control centres. The code follows the red lights indicating the presence of the train from section to section and from line to line as it switches from one to another. Usually the next two or three trains approaching the control area are displayed so that the signalman can see at a glance the order in which trains are running. Trains running very much out of course will be advised automatically by computer print-out or VDU from information recorded on computer in adjacent signalboxes or control centres.

Of course, the area controlled by an IECC or modern power signalling centre is usually large, covering many miles of line and numerous junctions.

Move now to the Scottish Highlands: the driver of a diesel locomotive calls up by radio to the control centre and asks the signalman for a token to proceed into the single-line section ahead. This is not the traditional metal token in the form of a large key, or staff which the driver or fireman had to collect by hand from the signalman, but an electronic token transmitted by radio to the driver's display panel on the locomotive. It is all carried out through data transmission by radio of information between the computer in the control centre and a microprocessor on board the locomotive or other traction unit.

During the 1930s the LNER pioneered not merely all-electric signalling

162

but route relay interlocking (in which relays provided the interlocking to prevent conflicting movements). Control at first was by thumb switches, and the turning of a single switch set a complete route from one signal to the next. The system was expanded after World War II by British Railways and used in a number of installations, especially York, Manchester and St Pancras. It was still used in the 1980s but at St Pancras it was replaced by the new West Hampstead signalling centre just before the decade opened, while York just about saw it out, being replaced by an IECC in 1989.

The next generation of signalling equipment, the entrance-exit system in which by pressing two buttons geographically positioned on a track diagram the signalman can set the route in a logical sequence rather than from clusters of thumb switches, was still being installed in conventional form well into the 1980s – with centres at Leicester, Westbury and Exeter among others. But the earliest major signalling control room of this pattern commissioned in the late 1940s at Liverpool Street was just being taken out of service and replaced by an IECC as the 1980s ended.

Whether of the one-control-switch type of panel or the entrance-exit pattern, the use of relay interlockings and the development of new technology in remote control systems during the 1950s and 1960s brought ever larger control areas taking over hundreds of miles and replacing numerous manual signalboxes. Edinburgh signalling centre for example controls much of South East Scotland looking after trains on the East Coast main line from the time they cross the border at Berwick until they reach Tayside. At one time the Southern Region was hoping to control the whole of its system from just thirteen signalboxes. It did not quite happen like that but the Brighton line from London is controlled from just three signalling centres at London Bridge (which also takes in much of the South and South East London suburbs), Victoria (which is actually at Clapham Junction, covering the remainder of the South and South East London network) and Three Bridges (which takes the rest of the South Coast route from Croydon right down to the English Channel).

While the control components and relays have gradually become smaller, the large number of tracks and extended distances have meant that the indication panels have become huge, with track diagrams spread round the whole of the operating room console. Not only is each track shown, divided up into different track circuit sections by different colours, but with routes set shown by white lights along the track concerned, changing to red representing a train on the section concerned, with signal indications as red (for danger) or green (for any of the proceed aspects) on the signal symbols along the tracks. The identity of trains is shown by the four-character alphanumerical code displayed in apertures along the diagram to correspond with the track circuit occupied by the train and moving along the track and from one line to another in step with the train. Now as already described in the latest IECCs this information is shown on a VDU while the entrance-exit buttons have been replaced by what looks like a typewriter keyboard and the relays by processors.

What of the signals themselves out on the line? For the last sixty years there have been two basic types of signal: semaphore and colour-light. Semaphore have been sub-divided into two, the lower and upper quadrant, both of course being horizontal for danger or caution. Both types were sub-divided into stop signals (red arm) and distant signals (yellow arm). In the 1980s the lower-quadrant type was still in use on the Western Region or other former Great Western lines because the Western signal engineers had earlier been sufficiently independent to follow former GW practice. The other railways gradually went over to the lighter upper-quadrant type from the 1920s.

Colour-light signals also began to make their appearance on the main-line railways (as distinct from urban or underground lines) from the 1920s and after World War II were adopted widely in connection with resignalling schemes and power operation. The basic colour-light code of red – danger, single yellow – caution be prepared to stop at the next signal ahead, double yellow – preliminary caution, be prepared to stop at the second signal ahead, and green – clear, remains to this day. In the late 1970s flashing single and double yellow aspects were added on high speed routes as advance warnings of diversions at a junction ahead on to a lower speed route, and flashing green aspects have been installed on the East Coast main line to provide an added aspect for the very high speeds of the future. Junction signals display a row of five white lights, usually above the main aspect, inclined or horizontally.

Over the last forty years automated aids have gradually been added to the older mechanical signalboxes and in-built to the later power signalling installations. Today in normal working signalmen cannot make mistakes in modern power signalboxes or IECCs. He may set up a wrong route: Exeter signalmen can (and have) sent an up London train booked to run up the Berks & Hants line, towards Bristol at Cogload Junction near Taunton. While inconvenient that was not unsafe.

Not so in the case of drivers. They can, and regrettably some do, make mistakes in passing signals at danger or reading the wrong signal, or exceeding speed limits or misjudging braking. No automation for them – yet. Sure, most drivers have had the automatic warning system, but it is installed on no more than two-thirds of the BR system some eighty years after the first experiments by the GWR. The GWR system, operated by mechanical contact between a shoe underneath the locomotive and a ramp between the rails approaching the distant signal, served its system well for seventy years. If the signal was at caution the shoe was raised and lowered as it passed over the ramp which triggered the warning sequence which sounded a horn; if the driver did not acknowledge it the brakes were applied automatically. If the signal was clear an electric current was transmitted from the ramp to the shoe which automatically countermanded the warning and sounded a bell briefly instead of the horn.

During the 1930s the LMS and LNER pioneered another form of ATC using the Hudd system which employed permanent and electromagnets between the rails to trigger the caution and clear indications. The LMS installed it on the London, Tilbury & Southend line, completed early in BR

days. During the 1950s BR developed a new standard type using the magnets of the Hudd system although placed together instead of spaced apart as on the LTS line, and the horn warning and bell clear indications of the GWR system, together with a dial indicator showing when a driver had acknowledged a warning or had passed a clear signal. The basic principle, though, had not changed from the original GWR idea, and it was still not employed at purely stop signals. As multiple-aspect colour-light signals began to be introduced widely there then arose the problem of what to do with the varying aspects because all three- and four-aspect colour-lights are stop signals in their own right but are also distants for the signal ahead. BR decided that the warning indication should be given for any aspect other than green because the automatic warning system as it was now called could not distinguish between red, single yellow and double yellow aspects. The clear indication bell was given only for a green aspect.

At first this was probably acceptable on the principal main lines where signals after resignalling during the 1960s and 1970s were usually spaced about a mile apart for four-aspects and 1½–2 miles in three-aspect areas for 100mph running.

On suburban routes with signals placed every few hundred yards trains in peak periods would encounter yellow or double yellow aspects every 20–30 seconds. On the dense Southern electric network in inner suburban areas headways between trains were such that is was normal for most rush-hour trains to be running on continuous single or double yellows. So said the Southern, we do not want AWS because there is a danger of drivers cancelling

As the 1980s opened, most large power signalboxes were of the 'entrance-exit' (NX) pattern where train descriptions and positions were displayed, and routes set up by pressing buttons, on the main panel. Saltley is typical of such boxes, controlling an area from Barnt Green and Leamington to Tamworth. At large centres (though not at Saltley) the station announcer is located in view of the panel. During the decade similar types, differing only in detail, were being commissioned at places such as London Victoria, Three Bridges, Westbury and Exeter.

165

A Chronology of Principal Developments in Signalling

Date	Development
1980	The London Midland Region completed the final stages of the West Hampstead resignalling scheme which controlled the lines from St Pancras to Sharnbrook, north of Bedford. The former LBSC and SEC routes from Victoria to be controlled from a new Victoria signal centre, located at Clapham Junction. The finishing touches were applied to the Highland line resignalling which involved re doubling between Blair Atholl and Dalwhinaie and the design of 'standard passing loop' signalling controlled from Aviemore on remaining single line sections between Kingussie and Culloden Moor. A change to the rules was introduced, requiring guards to see that platform starting signals were clear before giving the right away.
January	Contract placed with Westinghouse Signals for Brighton line resignalling, controlled by new box at Three Bridges. Replace 33 existing signalboxes between Norwood Junction, Selhurst and Brighton.
April	Train to signalbox radio equipment for St Pancras–Bedford Class 317 emus.
December	Radio link for existing Scottish Region tokenless block replaces pole route. Direct wire blown down by gales between Tain and Georgemas Junction, with microprocessor control supplied by ML Engineering Plymouth.
1981	
28 January	Resignalling from Westbury to Totnes costing £28m.
February	Work started on Colchester signalbox, part of a £15m resignalling scheme covering Colchester–Claydon (North of Ipswich).
May	Contract placed with GEC/GS for Cambridge resignalling to cover lines from Royston and Bishops Stortford to Fulbourne and Ely South, costing £7m.
June	BR, GEC/GS, and Westinghouse Signals to develop micro-processor-based solid state interlocking known as SSI. The first trial was at Leamington Spa in 1983, installed in parallel with conventional relay interlocking.
27–28 June	Victoria Stage 2 resignalling commissioned between Victoria and Norbury.
August	Final stage of Doncaster resignalling commissioned, and formally opened by BR Chairman Sir Peter Parker on 8 December 1981. Last semaphore signal on ECML between Doncaster and Kings Cross eliminated.
17–21 August	First stage of Salisbury resignalling between Grateley and Wilton commissioned. Fringe boxes will be Basingstoke, Eastleigh and Westbury.
15 November	Inauguration of Tyne & Wear Metro after royal opening on 6 November. Simplified colour-light signalling controlled from single control centre with automated route setting.
24 November	Completion of final stage of Edinburgh resignalling controlling 243 route miles, incl the ECML from Berwick to Cupar, also to Polmont, Ladybank, Hilton Junction, and Midcalder. Largest control area on BR.
November	Aberdeen resignalling complete between Dyce and Newtonhill; replaces 6 boxes and cost £2.1m.
	BR orders first production versions of traction immune jointless track circuit, the ML Engineering T1 21 style.
	Programme started to convert former GWR type lower quadrant signals to upper quadrant or colour light as renewals fall due on former GWR lines within LMR.
1982	
March	Contract placed with GEC/GS for Anglia stage 2 resignalling from Colchester to Sproughton and Westerfield Junction.
April	Assessment of radio electronic token block (RETB) to be undertaken by BR and Ultra Electronic Communications Ltd.
May	Final stage of Southampton resignalling commissioned.
December	Contract placed with ML Engineering for Maidstone East resignalling covering Borough Green to Ashford excl.
1983	
28 March	Driver only operation on St Pancras–Bedford emus with train to signalbox radio inaugurated after union resistance withdrawn.
25 June	First stage of Three Bridges resignalling commissioned on the Brighton line.

Date	Development
29 June	Leicester resignalling scheme authorised, covering 55 route miles from Sharnbrook to Loughborough.
	RETB authorised for Dingwall–Kyle of Lochalsh, to cost £415,000.
	Dundee resignalling authorised, to cost £2.5m.
July	Trials of computer based automatic route setting (ARS) system commissioned at Three Bridges signalling centre, to control Haywards Heath, Copyhold Junction, and Keymer Junction.
3 October	Selby diversion opened throughout between Templehirst Junction and Colton Junction providing a new length of ECML and purpose built for 125mph running, although speed initially limited to 60mph until 1984, with signalling controlled from York.
28 October	Tonbridge–Hastings line electrification and resignalling autho-rised, to be controlled from Tonbridge Robertsbridge, and Bo Peep Junction.
1984	
5 January	Contract placed with GEC/GS for Ayrshire resignalling as part of electrification, costing £3m.
May	Victoria signalling centre at Clapham Junction complete, covering 112 route miles and 270 track miles of the former SEC and LBSC routes. The largest English power signalling centre, exceeded only by Edinburgh.
14 May	First stage of Wesbury resignalling commissioned.
June	Contract placed with ML Engineering for Leicester resignalling covering 60 track miles, costing £4m.
6 July	RETB inaugurated between Dingwall and Kyle of Lochalsh.
September	Contract placed with GEC/GS for East Suffolk line RETB from Ipswich to Lowestoft controlled from Saxmundham.
1 October	Fire at existing Brighton signalbox destroys signalling cable. After emergency working with hand signalling, temporary reinstatement of Brighton box until takeover by Three Bridges in March 1985.
October	Contracts placed with Westinghouse Signals for a number of schemes including Crewe station, Kidsgrove, Guide Bridge (to control Manchester–Glossop–Hadfield) and renewal at Manchester Piccadilly. Discussions under way regarding fifth aspect for 140mph East Coast main line services now being planned. Suggested that transponder could be used to trigger target speed display in cab.
December	Authorisation for £32.5m Waterloo resignalling with boundaries at Berrylands, Bookham, Boxhill, Chessington, Putney and branches.
	Contract placed with Westinghouse signals for Bolton resignalling worth £½m.
1985	
February	Last West of England main line stage of Westbury resignalling complete to Athelney.
23/24 February	Final stage of Cambridge area resignalling complete, the first stage having been commissioned in October 1982.
April	Resignalling commissioned in stages to January 1986 between Tonbridge and Bo Peep Junction (St Leonards) as part of electrification.
	Final stage of Three Bridges signalling centre complete with conversion of Redhill area. The whole of London–Brighton line now controlled by three signalling centres at London Bridge, Victoria (Clapham Junction) and Three Bridges. Total cost of latter two schemes £120m (including SEC lines) and 70 old signalboxes eliminated.
	Contract placed with GEC/GS for Inverness resignalling to include SSI.
May	First stage of Exeter resignalling commissioned, the last major conventional relay interlocking scheme to be installed.
2 June–21 July	Crewe station and approaches shut for seven weeks for 'big bang' complete remodelling and resignalling from new Crewe signalling centre.
September	Contract placed with GEC/GS for final stages of Anglia resignalling controlled from Colchester, between Mellis, Norwich, Whittlingham Junction and Wymondham. Worth £3.3m and due for completion May 1987.

Date	Development
	Contract between ML Engineering and Vaughan Systems and Programming Ltd for colour vdu screens for train describer system at Leicester.
1986	
May	Contract with Westinghouse signals for £1.5m resignalling on south coast line between Portslade and Angmering controlled by Lancing for completion in 1987.
27 June	Leicester resignalling stage 1 commissioned. Final stage completed on 7 December 1987 brings Leicester control area to Sharnbrook–Loughborough N Jct. Total cost £14.4m.
June	Resignalling on Oxted line in hand at a cost of £1m. Oxted SB will have SSI.
August	Authorisation of York resignalling with SSI at a cost of £18m as a prelude to ECML electrification.
	Work starts on resignalling Euston–Watford dc electric line to cost £2.94m.
28 September	Ayr line resignalling complete.
1987	
May	Final stage of Exeter area resignalling complete with Exeter controlling from Athelney to Totnes. Last semaphore signals on West of England main line between Paddington and Plymouth eliminated, although semaphores will remain at Bradford Junction between Westbury and Trowbridge until 1989, and a few remain between Plymouth and Penzance.
June	RETB to be installed between Inverness and Dingwall.
October	300 SR emus to be fitted with train to signalbox radio for speech and data transmission.
November	Contract with Westinghouse Signals for SSI equipment for Liverpool Street–Bethnal Green resignalling, completion in May 1989.
December	Contract placed with Westinghouse Signals for RETB for Cambrian Coast line controlled from Machynlleth. Completion and commissioning takes place between Shrewsbury–Aberystwyth/Pwllheli on 24 October 1988.
7 December	First stage of RETB commissioned on West Highland line between Fort William and Mallaig. Later stages completed between Helensburgh and Oban in March 1988, and Upper Tyndrum–Fort William on 19 May 1988.
December	Contracts placed with CAP Industry Ltd for IECCs for York and Liverpool Street.
1988	
February	Contract placed with Westinghouse Signals for train to signalbox radio for Euston–Northampton services.
April	Contract for train to signalbox radio for SR Central and Eastern services to be implemented in stages from 1989.
	Contract with Westinghouse for SSI for resignalling between Hurst Green and Uckfield to be controlled by Oxted.
June	Network SouthEast announces total route modernisation for Marylebone–Aylesbury/High Wycombe routes including £11m for resignalling, with IECCs by Vaughan Systems & Programming Ltd. Work to start in Autumn 1988.
August	Electrification to Leeds as part of ECML completed to allow test running. Flashing green signal/aspects introduced between New England (Peterborough) and Stoke (Grantham) for trials at over 125mph. Flashing Green denotes that the train may run up to 140mph, steady green that the train may run up to 125mph (or slow down to 125mph from speeds over that limit).
1989	
24–28 March	Liverpool Street resignalling with IECC commissioned.
7 June	Mersey PTE agreed to spend £20.35m on centralised control system for Merseyrail Northern and Wirral lines including resignalling with supervision from a single control centre.
13 July	Rt Hon Bruce Millan, Commission member of the EEC hands over cheque for £19.5m to BR from European Development Fund towards the total cost of £31m of the Newcastle resignalling scheme, to be commissioned in October 1990.
July	Railway Inspectorate unhappy with installation of single lead junctions in place of double junctions until the findings of the Bellgrove Junction collision inquiry are assessed.
	Huddersfield area resignalling plans costing £2.5m announced.
23 November	Network SouthEast contract with Westinghouse Signals for resignalling SE main line from Chislehurst to Folkestone from new control centre at Ashford with SSI at a cost of £20.8m. To be complete by 1993.

warnings at yellow after yellow and doing the same at a red signal and forgetting the fact that the signal is showing red. You will have AWS, said the British Railways Board, and although the Southern tried to develop an improved AWS which showed the actual signal aspect on the driver's control desk the cost was too high. Thus AWS came to the Southern as well as the other regions. And so, too, have the accidents caused by drivers unconsciously cancelling an AWS warning at a red signal and running past the signal into collision, not just on the SR but on other regions as well.

Certainly the lack of positive train control to stop a driver running past a signal at danger or exceeding a speed limit is the weak link in the safety chain. The Dutch and some other mainland European railways have had some form of full automation to prevent driving errors over the last two decades, and certainly the technology exists in Britain. For the last twenty years London Transport has had a fully automated railway, the Victoria Line, in which the driver, or train operator as he is known, does nothing more than press the start button after which the train proceeds under total automation. More recently the Docklands Light Railway has opened with its fully automated computer operation of trains. By the end of 1980s BR was developing a new automatic train protection (ATP) system for the higher speeds of the future which fulfils the automatic supervision of a driver's actions and will prevent signal over-runs. Trials are to take place as part of resignalling on the Chiltern line from London, and the Paddington–Bristol route during the early 1990s. Hopefully it will be compatible with systems across the Channel so that with the completion of the Channel Tunnel in 1993 there will not be a British system and a differing French system on the same train which will do nothing to enhance safety but much to add to costs.

Whatever automation is provided signalling safety is still in the hands of those who make, install, and maintain the equipment. No one before that December morning in 1988 could have contemplated a train correctly running by a signal showing a proceed aspect and suddenly finding another train standing in its path a short distance ahead. Yet the Clapham Junction accident, in which there was heavy loss of life, showed graphically what can happen when careless installation work on new signalling left a redundant but still live wire dangling in contact with an in-use relay terminal, causing a signal to show a false aspect. No one could contemplate it happening because the standards of British signal engineering are so high. Indeed only once before, and that half a century earlier, had a similar false indication caused a collision – when a technician made a wiring mistake on the London Underground. Just two mistakes fifty years apart but the second was far more devastating, not merely because it resulted in a major train accident (among the top half-dozen ever on the Southern) but because it showed that whatever

Clouds of smoke rise from torches as rescue workers separate the two commuter trains that collided during the morning rush hour at Clapham, London's busiest train junction, on 12 December 1988. Thirty-five people were reported killed and at least 150 others injured when the trains collided and a third train ploughed through the wreckage.

relay, processor, or other equipment is used in the safety chain it is only as safe as it is made to be. With all the 1980s technology safety cannot be one hundred per cent, any more than it was when the first block instruments and interlocking were devised in the middle of the last century. But with higher speeds and more traffic it is essential that lessons from the 1980s are learned and applied to the full.

Accidents of the 1980s
Official Statistics

Year	Total number of train accidents	Passenger train collisions*	Passenger train derailments	Passengers in train accidents killed	Passengers in train accidents major injuries
1980	930	13	28	–	27
1981	1014	18	35	4	12
1982	998	15	23	–	3
1983	1225	17	25	2	9
1984	1359	17	33	18	28
1985	1240	17	30	–	31
1986	1171	19	34	8	44
1987	1164	20	20	3	13
1988	1330	18	28	34	75

* Excluding bufferstop collisions; includes collisions between passenger and non passenger trains
Figures for 1989 had not been published as this book went to press

Principal accidents on BR caused by driver or signalling error

Date	Location	Accident	Killed (*staff)	Responsibility	Cause	Recommendation
1980						
27.4	Portsmouth	Collision 2 passgr trains	–	Driver	AWS ackd, passed signal at danger	Signal sighting improved. AWS magnet moved
5.6	Hyndland	Collision passgr train/ ECS	–	Signalman & driver	Conflicting instructions in fault conditions. Driver failed to run at caution	
1981						
5.4	Kirby Cross	Collision passgr train/ ECS	–	Driver	Passed semaphore signal at danger at single line passing loop	Additional controls on home signal
9.6	Chester	Derailment passgr train	–	Signalman	Reversed points under train but electrical fault had removed locking protection	Combination of 2 errors by signalman at same time as 2 earth faults; unlikely to be repeated

Date	Location	Accident	Killed (*staff)	Respon-sibility	Cause	Recommen-dation
18.6	Parks Bridge Jct	Collision 2 passgr trains	–	Driver	Passed signal at danger. No AWS	AWS to be provided
13.11	Bromley Jct	Collision 2 passgr trains	–	Driver	Passed signal at danger. No AWS	AWS to be provided
11.12	Seer Green	Collision passgr train/ECS	1★ 3	Signal-man & driver	Driver wrongly instructed to pass signal at danger in snow but failed to run at caution	More precise definition of 'caution', staff training improve-ments etc
1983						
23.11	Paddington	Derailment sleeping car train	–	Driver	Excessive speed at permanent speed restriction	Revision of conditions under which advanced warning indicators & AWS pro-vided to include cascaded restrictions
1984						
24.6	Morpeth	Derailment sleeping car train	–	Driver but possible medical condi-tion and alcohol effect	Excessive speed at permanent speed restriction	As Paddington (see above) but also possibility of full cab signalling as automatic train pro-tection (ATP)
11.10	Wembley	Collision passgr/Freight-liner	3	Tran-sient medical condi-tion of driver	AWS ackd, signal passed at danger	More effective AWS; revised medical arrangements
4.12	Eccles	Collision passgr train	2 1★	Driver	Semaphore signal passed at danger. No AWS	AWS to be provided in the area
1985						
31.5	Battersea Park	Collision 2 passgr trains	–	Driver	AWS ackd, signal passed at danger	More effective AWS at danger signals
26.9	Paisley	Collision passgr/freight	–	Driver	Semaphore signal passed at danger	None, but BRB already investigating signals passed at danger

170

Date	Location	Accident	Killed (*staff)	Respon- sibility	Cause	Recommen- dation
6.11	Haywards Heath	Collision 2 passgr trains	–	Leaves on track	Train braking in- effective because of wheelslide	Better management of lineside vegetation
1986						
9.3	Chinley	Collision passgr train/ 2LEs	1*	Signal- man	During fault conditions signalman pumped points by hand but failed to lock	Better training
19.9	Colwich	Collision 2 passgr trains	1*	Driver	AWS ackd, but signal passed at danger. Flashing yellow junction aspects not understood by driver	Signalling alterations to flashing yellow aspect; better advice of alterations and better emergency braking
16.10	Kensal Green	Collision 2 passgr trains	–	Driver	Excessive speed after passing automatic call-on signal	Minor details; line since resignalled
1987						
24.3	Frome	Collision Freight/ passgr	–	Driver	AWS ackd, signal passed at danger	Could have been pre- vented by Automatic train protection
1988						
12.12	Clapham Jct	Double collision 2 passgr/ ECS	34 1*	S&T Staff	Redundant but live wire short circuited relay terminal and caused signal to show false aspect	‡
1989						
4.3	Purley	Collision 2 passgr trains	5	Driver	AWS ackd, signal passed at danger	+
6.3	Bellgrove Jct (Glasgow)	Collision 2 passgr trains	1*	Driver	AWS ackd, signal passed at danger	+

Note ‡. 93 specific recommendations including improved installation and testing procedures for resignalling work, specific management responsibilities, training, the adoption of on-train data recorders, train to signallman radio, rapid installation of automatic train protection, public address on trains, and better command, relations and communication with emergency services.

Note +. The official reports into these accidents had not been published as this book closed for press.

14
THE TENUOUS LINK
WITH STEAM

'WHO will rid me of this base turbulent priest?' Thomas à Becket was murdered in Canterbury Cathedral in 1170; it took BR until Guy Fawkes' day 1988 finally to remove steam from its timetable. The two-foot-gauge one hundred per cent steam Vale of Rheidol section based on Aberystwyth had led a Damoclean existence ever since the piratical Bobby Lawrence then general manager of the London Midland Region had attempted to sell it off in 1968; he retired hurt after entering the fray against the Welsh and the unions. Bob Reid's cohorts were stronger and the sword made as clean a cut as possible with the line going to the owners of the successfully entrepreneurial Brecon Mountain Railway.

But links with steam remain – all with the private sector and neatly packaged into two parts – with SLOA (and when BR feels like it direct with the private locomotive owners) plus the preserved/tourist lines. Who would have thought a few short years ago that 'The train now standing in platform No 1 is a through British Rail charter train from Manchester to Bridgnorth via Kidderminster'? By no means common place this was a possible scene in the decade where private railways were physically linked to British Rail via an operational connection. In an uncertain world of fast-moving change such operations have helped to strengthen the bonds which exist at many levels between British Rail and the preservation movement.

Take three examples; the vibrant Severn Valley Railway Plc from Kidderminster to Bridgnorth led by the indomitable Michael Draper has countless members whose daily bread is provided by BR and whose skills freely given in their spare time, have helped to establish that scene of professionalism which pervades the railway – and in the 1980s the huge task of building the Kidderminster connection. Like many sister tourist lines the SVR is also well into the field of joint ticket sales and promotion; it helps towards the vital positive cash flow and the hard thinking necessary to the railway tourist industry for ultimately it is the passenger who decides whether any operation survives or dies.

The Dart Valley Railway Plc in Devon also has connections with BR – at Totnes and Paignton. Each tells a different story. The Dart Valley section from Totnes to Buckfastleigh has access to the town only via the BR bridge over the Dart into Totnes station. For nigh on twenty years this was refused by BR but in 1985 Bill Bradshaw, then GM of the Western Region paved the way – in the end, sadly, to no avail. It was killed off by cost. To run those few hundred yards all DVR coaching stock and locos had to be inspected by

BR engineers on a 'daily exam' basis. They also had to be registered leading to other costly examinations from time to time. This and the fact that BR also demanded a pilot driver and guard (sent up by taxi for each operation) put the scheme out of court – and the Dart Valley section out on a limb.

The Kingswear line is able to receive trains from BR; these provide additional revenue but are few and far between.

A success story of co-operation and the linking of traffic has been in North Wales where the Festiniog Railway, one of Britain's finest and best run tourist lines, meets BR both at Porthmadog, on the Cambrian Coast, and Blaenau Ffestiniog, the terminus of the Conwy Valley branch from Llandudno Junction. Called the Ffestiniog Link the two lines share a new central station at Blaenau opened in May 1982 by Lord Tonypandy. They provide a ride (not possible since 1939) over forty miles across Snowdonia through some of the most beautiful scenery in Britain and bring valuable traffic to each party.

Steam can also be seen over BR's tracks from time to time; all of it provided by private owners who need to comply with rigid standards. From Crewe to Holyhead, Marylebone to Derby via Birmingham, Newport to Shrewsbury, Chester and Crewe, from the shadow of Ben Nevis to Mallaig, steam's

Vale of Rheidol, BR's last regular steam operation. No 9 Prince of Wales *comes round the curve below Nantyronen with the 11.40 from Aberystwyth to Devils Bridge on the Spring Gala day in May 1986. The engine is in today's interpretation of the original Vale of Rheidol livery.*

heritage, held in trust by today's private railways and steam centres has become part of a way of life. An expensive part and one becoming more difficult as year succeeds year. BR is now training volunteer crews in steam-engine practice. It runs the Mallaig operations itself, and from time to time others such as the Marylebone to Stratford upon Avon Sunday lunch trains and specials laid on by InterCity director Dr John Prideaux. To be fair the acknowledged hire fees are always paid to the locomotive owners but even so owning and running a steam engine on BR's tracks is only a business for those with hearts of gold and nerves of steel.

In the whole decade 1985 stands out; it was the year of Great Western 150 – a century and a half to be celebrated. The Western Region entered into this with gusto though other regions were not so sure. Under general manager Bill Bradshaw and later Sidney Newey a special committee was set up to plan the celebrations which were to be based on a Swindon Works bonanza; engines, stock, ephemera, society stands, the lot. Led by David Pattison, a retired senior WR officer specially appointed for the purpose, the committee included Tony Hall-Patch from the Science Museum (parent to the NRM), the railway officers involved, and the relevant locomotive owners/organisations. It got off to a good start. Sadly other BR management had conflicting ideas; right in the middle of it all came the announcement of the impending closure of Swindon Works. The men went on strike and the exhibition out of the window.

But all was not lost – the planned steam runs still took place and by and large these were a success. The epics were the Bristol–Plymouth and Swindon–Gloucester trips using a King, two Castles, a Hall and a Manor. There was a debacle when a Hall and a Castle stalled on Dainton – poor coal was one of the excuses. In fact no down runs to Plymouth were completed but return trips behind No 5051 *Drysllwyn Castle* and No 7029 *Clun Castle* made amends. The Swindon–Gloucester affairs ran well and gave a great deal of satisfaction. The sesqui-centenary was also celebrated by steam trains from Birmingham to Stratford, Swansea to Carmarthen and by an epic run in Cornwall. It was to have been made by the famous No 3440 *City of Truro* but unfortunately it was not restored to running order in time. Nevertheless a compensatory run took place later in the year from Gloucester to Newport.

Late in the afternoon of 6 September 1985 the crowds began to form on the high ground looking down on Brunel's great bridge over the Tamar, gazing across the water towards Saltash on the western bank. They heard a now strange whistle and in the distance they saw a feather of steam rising from a polished brass safety valve saddling a gleaming green boiler; more steam drifted over a rake of chocolate-and-cream coaches. It was a picture long forgotten by most and one not witnessed for over two decades, almost a generation. The train wound its way from Truro, St Austell, Par, Lostwithiel and Liskeard. A puff of white steam from the chimney visible seconds before the sound of its exhaust, carried across the wide river and No 7029 *Clun Castle* moved her train slowly but majestically and rolled it over the great span high above the water.

Private line working into BR station. 1600 Class 0-6-0PT No 1638 arrives at Totnes BR station with the 11.15 ex-Buckfastleigh on Easter Saturday 1985.

BR working on to a private railway. Hertfordshire Rail Tours' Torbay Express from Derby to Kingswear arrives at the Devonshire terminus, with No 43095 Heaton leading, on 14 March 1988. It was the first time an HST had been over the Torbay and Dartmouth Railway.

1982 saw the opening of a new interchange station at Blaenau Ffestiniog between BR and the newly extended Festiniog Railway. Here passengers from a BR excursion (including the SLOA Pullman rake) change to the FR train hauled by the double Fairlie locomotive Merddin Emrys *in June 1982.*

Out of the last great arch it came, the copper rim to the Castle's chimney just catching a fleeting ray of sunshine, round the curve to disappear towards Plymouth North Road station.

Steam and BR are uneasy bedfellows but slowly a pattern is emerging for the future, more formal than before and less fun for sure but in the end it has to be survival that matters.

Operational needs dictate professionalism so it is not altogether surprising that the senior management of the majority of private railways and steam centres is in the hands of people who have established careers in the real world of industry and the professions, a development which is not entirely strange to BR itself.

Great Western 150 (i). The magnificent sight of Castles double heading the Great Western Ltd on the up fast line near Tiverton Junction on 8 September 1985. The locomotives concerned are Nos 7029 Clun Castle *and 5051* Drysllwyn Castle.

Great Western 150 (ii). No 7029 Clun Castle *comes across the Royal Albert Bridge from Cornwall into Devon en route from Truro to Plymouth. It was the first steam locomotive to make the crossing in twenty-one years.*

A photograph taken prior to the 1980s but a scene which could be said to be typical of the earlier days of the decade before the electrification of the East Coast Main Line. York station looking south with No 4498 Sir Nigel Gresley — one of the most frequent performers over BR's metals at the head of a steam special.

Eric Treacy/Millbrook House Collection

15
THE CHANNEL TUNNEL

IN the event, the 1980s ended with work at full speed on the long-dreamed-of Channel Tunnel though in the 1970s completion had been promised for around 1980, and picking up the pieces after the shattering blow of January 1975 when the British Labour Government pulled the plug had been a slow process.

It began with BR and the SNCF working out in some detail a so-called 'mousehole' concept – a single-line rail tunnel to BR gauge that would link their two systems at minimum cost. It would employ a 'tidal flow' principle of flights of trains in one direction, probably for a period of two hours, followed by flights in the opposite direction. The advantages, in addition to minimal cost, included avoiding hostility from the roll-on, roll off ferry ship operators, since road vehicle traffic (except for some Motorail cars) would continue to move by sea; and using the existing Southern Region infrastructure should avoid stirring up the sort of environmental protest that had been vocal in 1974.

However, the more the mousehole was studied, the more complications appeared. First of all, for safety reasons a second or service tunnel would probably have to be provided, at substantial cost. Then, it would be short-sighted if the mousehole were not built so that at some future date it could if desirable accommodate trains of the Continental loading gauge, again increasing the cost. Lastly, there was the Conservative Government's objection to public-sector investment on the one hand, yet on the other serious doubts whether private finance could be obtained for a scheme that would not exploit the highly profitable roll-on roll-off road vehicle traffic.

The political climate was however changing by the early 1980s. In September 1981 President Mitterrand and Mrs Thatcher jointly expressed enthusiasm for the idea of a fixed link. Once again the creaking governmental machine was set in motion, covering the ground that had been so thoroughly trodden in the 1960s and 1970s. It would be tedious to describe here the work of study groups and working parties, with reports by experts that, more or less, merely reinforced earlier conclusions. There was also the constant campaigning by tunnel opponents such as the Dover Harbour Board, European Ferries and Sealink UK, the last-named having had to be sold off by BR in 1984 on government instructions. In 1985 these interested parties, working together under the name of 'Flexilink', promoted an intensive anti-Tunnel propaganda campaign that included scaremongering on subjects such as fire risks and even rabies. It worthily carried on the tradition of Sir Garnet

Wolseley and the Duke of Cambridge who in 1882 opposed a tunnel on the grounds that it might enable some new Napoleon to fight a second battle of Waterloo, but on English soil!

By this time a British 'Channel Tunnel Group' with strong financial backing had been formed with an equally strong French partner, 'France-Manche', to promote what was, in most essentials, the scheme abandoned in 1975, though this time without the dedicated high-speed rail link which had been in an advanced state of planning when cancelled. Inevitably, the politicians called for alternative proposals: three main ones emerged, all of which provided some form of drive-through roadway. This was the principle reported to be preferred by Mrs Thatcher; it had been exhaustively examined in the 1960s and then decisively rejected in favour of a tunnel based on rail technology but providing, as well as an international rail connection, a 'rolling motorway' using Ro-Ro shuttle trains to carry road vehicles – cars, coaches and heavy lorries.

The new contenders were 'Eurobridge' (backed by British Steel), 'Euroroute' and 'Channel Expressway'. Euroroute revived an idea first put forward in Napoleon's time by Albert Mathieu-Favier, for an artificial island in mid-Channel. Its proposal was for *two* artificial islands, with descending spiral roadways leading to an immersed tube tunnel linking them under water, but with bridges connecting them to the shore. A 'mousehole' rail tunnel was also included.

The last project, Channel Expressway, was something of a curiosity, since it was sponsored by the owner of Sealink UK – maybe a sort of death-bed repentance? Envisaging trains using tracks sunk in the hard shoulder of an underwater motorway, it received short shrift.

Finally on 20 January 1986 President Mitterrand and Mrs Thatcher, meeting in Lille, announced support for the CTG/France-Manche scheme. Mrs Thatcher's preference for a drive-through tunnel was appeased by an agreement that studies for such a project would follow the completion of the rail-based tunnel. A treaty was signed in Canterbury the following month, and at last a Channel Tunnel Bill, introduced in April 1986, received Royal Assent on 23 July 1987. The next month it was announced that already fifty international banks had joined to guarantee the financing of the work, and the British and French promoters adopted a common title – Eurotunnel plc in Britain and Eurotunnel SA in France.

The railways had collaborated closely with the Channel Tunnel Group in both the technology and economic assessments. But their position was weaker than it had been in the 1970s, for now Eurotunnel, with its powerful private financing backers, decided to be, in effect, a separate railway company, operating the shuttle trains itself. The British and French railways would be merely users of the tunnel for their own trains, paying appropriate tolls. However, an agreement was reached for half the train paths to be reserved for the international passenger and freight trains.

The SNCF promptly obtained the French Government's support for the construction of the TGV Nord as France's third high-speed route. No such encouragement came from the British Government, and BR had to tell the SNCF and SNCB that there was no prospect of operating between Paris, Brussels and London except with trains conforming to the British loading gauge, so special dedicated rolling stock and locomotives would be required. Locomotives for through working would require to be poly-current – 750V DC third rail, 25kV AC and 3,000V DC overhead current collection, for running in England, France and Belgium respectively.

Yet BR's traffic prospects arising from the tunnel were so attractive that government approval could not be withheld from the investment essential to cope with it, though on a minimal scale. This comprises the locomotives and rolling stock; a London terminal; a maintenance and servicing depot for international trains; transit centres in the London area for traffic to and from the provinces, both passengers and freight; a freight holding yard near the tunnel terminal at Ashford; and an international passenger station on the British side of the tunnel. The London passenger terminal is to be at Waterloo, provided by an ingenious remodelling scheme. The wide roadway between platforms 11 and 12, no longer used by taxicabs, is being taken up by additional platforms to accommodate trains formerly using the 'Windsor side' of the station. That part is to be reconstructed as 'Waterloo International', with platform lengthening at the country end, and a wide range of facilities.

Connecting Waterloo with the existing boat-train routes to Folkestone is being achieved by building a chord line or 'creep-up' from the Windsor lines at Stewart's Lane, where the tracks from Victoria pass over the main lines from Waterloo. As far as this point the international trains will share tracks with the local traffic on the 'Windsor lines' where there are three tracks for most of the way. The former 'Chatham' line from Victoria is being given some relief by connections to the under-utilised South London line which parallels it for part of the way.

The various boat-train routes between Victoria and Folkestone will all be used; they include the Catford loop between Brixton and Shortlands, and the line from Swanley via Maidstone East to Ashford, as well as the No 1 route which uses the Chislehurst curves to reach the former South Eastern main line via Tonbridge. The best and fastest route is via Tonbridge and Ashford and over the 26½ miles between those points it can be brought up to 100mph standard. Even so, quickest journeys from Waterloo to the tunnel cannot be less than 70 minutes. Any other route imposes a time penalty.

The servicing and maintenance of the international trains has been planned at a depot on the West London line near Old Oak Common, on semi-derelict open ground. To reach this depot a disused spur connecting the SR's Windsor lines with the West London from the Waterloo direction must be reinstated. It seems to have been last used for regular passenger services (from Waterloo to Richmond via Kensington Addison Road and Hammersmith) in 1916; the tracks were lifted in 1937.

Trainloads from major Continental centres to British industrial areas – whether in wagons or containers – should be highly remunerative for BR.

Most freight will pass through Willesden, where there are good connections both for depots in the London region and for ongoing traffic to the Midlands and North. Willesden will not however be itself an Inland Customs Depot where seals on wagons and containers are broken and clearance takes place: that will be performed at major inland destination points, details of which were preliminarily published in December 1989.

Freight trains emerging from the tunnel will first call at Dolland's Moor, a yard being constructed on the north side of the SR main line, just before Saltwood tunnel. Here locomotives will be changed, and customs inspection of seals on wagons and containers can take place. Outbound freight wagons will be subject to a safety inspection before entering the tunnel. Much freight will reach the West London line via Tonbridge, Redhill and the Brighton main line, since the more generous loading gauge here avoids the constraints on passing ISO containers 8ft 6in high which afflict the former South Eastern main line with its tunnels at Polhill, Sevenoaks and elsewhere – and also its heavy track occupation.

While many London–Paris and London–Brussels expresses will be non-stop to and from Waterloo International, an important intermediate station, to be called Ashford International is to be built for passengers wishing to change here into local services, or to continue their journey by car (a large car park will be provided).

The maximum possible train service will be four passenger and two freight trains, each way, per hour, while during the morning and evening peaks of business travel, only *three* international passenger trains, and *no* freight trains, can be accepted by the Southern Region – a serious constraint.

The basic service will be the daytime trains to Paris and Brussels, in about 3¼ hours to Paris and 3 hours to Brussels. In addition there will be a service of trains, some with sleeping cars, between centres such as Edinburgh, Manchester, Birmingham, Leeds and Paris/Brussels. These will travel via the West London line, which will be improved (especially the Chelsea river bridge) and electrified, to the south of Olympia at 750V DC, and at 25kV AC to the north of that station. Since the SNCF have obtained authority to link Paris-Nord with TGV Sud-Est by a line around Paris, there is the possibility of continuous high-speed travel without change of train to the South of France, Switzerland and Italy.

The new international trains will be much like the TGVs, but built to the smaller British loading gauge. They are designed for speeds in France and Belgium of up to 300km/hr (185m/hr) but in England the maximum will be 160km/hr (100m/hr), and that only between Ashford and Tonbridge. The work of building 30 trains (14 for BR, 13 for the SNCF and 3 for the SNCB), at a total cost of around £500 million, was tendered for by a consortium of two British, three French and two Belgian companies, the British partners being GEC-Alsthom and Brush Electrical. Towards the end of 1989 it was announced that contracts for building the trains had been signed. The fleet has been collectively termed the 'Three Capitals' trains, since they principally will link London, Paris and Brussels.

Channel Tunnel. Overall view of the Shakespeare Cliff working site with the main line between Dover and Folkestone to the right.

Contracts were also placed in 1989 for the fleet of 'Euroshuttle' trains providing the 'rolling motorway' through the tunnel. This fleet comprises 40 locomotives, 252 car-carrying or 'tourist' vehicles (including loading and unloading wagons at each end of a train) and a similar number of lorry-carrying single-deck wagons. Each train will be powered by a locomotive at each end.

The cost of the 'Euroshuttle' fleet provided Eurotunnel with an unpleasant surprise, being well above the estimates partly due to added safety requirements. About the same time as this was announced, the fact emerged of serious disagreements between Eurotunnel and its consortium of contractors (five British and five French) who are actually executing the work. (The consortium is known as Trans-Manche-Link, or TML for short.) The principal argument was over the final costs to completion, for which Eurotunnel would be liable. Students of railway history will not find this surprising; contractors have constantly asked for payments to be increased, usually alleging changes in design, delay in receiving instructions, and increases in the cost of materials and labour as their justification. In turn, railways have complained of delays or unsatisfactory performance by contractors.

In the case of the tunnel, prolonged negotiations were in progress at the end of the decade, but the extent of the additional finance required for completion, probably around £2billion still had to be determined. There was however no suggestion that the tunnel would be abandoned: the boring machines had already completed many kilometres of excavation, and the Stock Market still valued the shares of Eurotunnel far above their issue price.

The actual digging of the tunnel in 1989 was proceeding at a rate that gave no serious grounds for postponing the contract opening date of June 1993. The French had, as anticipated, encountered some difficult ground for the first few kilometres excavated by the service tunnel, leading the way for the rail running tunnels, out from the French coastline; and the British had to overcome some 'teething' problems with a rail tunnel boring machine. But the forecast breakthrough and union of the two service tunnels was still expected in November 1990.

British Rail meanwhile was active. As well as commissioning the rolling stock, work started on the construction of Waterloo International, as daily commuters into the station observed in the second half of 1989. Site levelling for the Dolland's Moor depot was well advanced, and first preparations for work on Ashford International station started. But, while the planning for the 1993 situation was being translated into physical works, this can only be an interim or short-term strategy. It is clear that, soon after the tunnel opens, there will be a pressing need for much better route and terminal capacity.

There may be disputes as to just when this will become critical. Eurotunnel and some consultants think it will be sooner than 1998, while BR have considered 2000 a more probable date. It is not just a question of lopping half an hour off the journey time to Paris and Brussels (though that will be valuable in a time-sensitive market), but of capacity.

That there is interest from private industry was more than clear at the end of 1989 when arguments for and against rival routes across Kent raged in the media. As the decade ended, BR was for a high-speed railway that will have Waterloo and King's Cross as its London termini. King's Cross was chosen because it offers direct links with two main lines to the North, and the Thameslink cross-river services – and also three Underground lines. It was seen as part of a vast new development planned by the London Regeneration Consortium for an area (much of it semi-derelict) between and to the north of St Pancras and King's Cross main-line stations. There was however strong opposition to BR's preferred route through Kent, many people believing a more easterly route avoiding South London and with a major new terminal at Stratford would be more appropriate. BR were doing their best to appease angry protestors and politicians along their preferred Kent route; for example, compensation was guaranteed at full market value disregarding the effects the railway would have on property values, though many experts thought the scale of potential damage had been exaggerated. But BR did not deposit its Bill as it had planned for November 1989 and the decade ended in uncertainty so far as an upgraded route is concerned.

The Channel Tunnel will essentially be the story of the 1990s. Given there is no catastrophe (economic or otherwise), the 1980s ended with the fair certainty that the tunnel will be opened in 1993, with through seating and sleeping-car trains from many parts of Britain and an injection of freight traffic that could be the chief salvation of BR at the century's end. But in announcing details of the likely new trains on opening (well ahead of the likely completion of any new route through Kent about which arguments were set to continue well into 1990) the BR chairman once again emphasised that trains will be run for profit, not for the public's general benefit. That the public (though still confused between what will happen on opening and when a new high-speed link across Kent is completed) were beginning to realise that the Channel Tunnel was becoming a reality was demonstrated by the high-pitched lobbying from the regions eager not to be left out of the economic miracle steadily foreseen.

16
CHRONOLOGY

1980
February 1 First refurbished Kent Coast EMU exhibited.

May 23 Rainhill 150th anniversary cavalcade.

July 14 Government announces 'progressive privatisation' of BR and subsidiaries.

October 12 Barmouth viaduct closed for repairs to seaworm damage.

October 23 First trials with Leyland Lightweight Experimental Vehicle (LEV).

December 4 Operating problems force postponement of APT investment plans.

December 8 Edinburgh–Glasgow main line reopened after complex repairs to Falkirk High tunnel.

1981
January 2 BR proposes 'half cost railways' with cheaper stock, reduced manpower and simplified signalling.

February 11 Report advocates electrification to Edinburgh by 1994, Bristol 1997 and Penzance 1997.

May 22 Barmouth bridge reopened after £500,000 repairs.

July 1 BR withdraws from loss-making collection and delivery business.

July 18 Manchester–Sheffield (Woodhead) route closed to all traffic.

July 29 Special trains for wedding of Prince and Princess of Wales.

August 28 Salisbury (Laverstock) loop reopened after 122 years.

September 30 New Plymouth HST depot opened.

October 3 Last run of LNER-design EMUs out of London Liverpool Street.

November 6 Tyne & Wear Metro officially opened.

December 7 APT briefly enters revenue service.

1982
January 2 Last BR runs by Class 55 'Deltic' locos on King's Cross–Edinburgh specials.

January 10 Mark 3 sleepers introduced on East Coast main line.

May 14 New InterCity station opened at Milton Keynes.

May 25 First run by restored privately owned VSOE Pullmans.

October 4 First timetabled HSTs work on Midland main line to St Pancras.

October 16 Cambridge power box commissioned.

December 9 First Class 58 locomotive delivered to Railfreight.

1983
May 16 New Glasgow–Harwich *European* service.

July 11 Moorgate–Bedford electrification inaugurated.

September 4 Last run in service of ex-SR 4-SUB unit.

September 19 Robert Reid replaces Sir Peter Parker as BR chairman.

September 24 New ECML Selby diversion opened.

November 23 Paddington derailment; loco 50041 arrives on its side.

December 15 Closure of Settle & Carlisle Line announced.

1984
January 5 First on-train public telephone on Paddington–Swansea HST.

February 13 Western Region headquarters moved to Swindon.

March 15 Marylebone station closure announced.

May 1 Victoria signalling centre opened.

May 14 New Gatwick Express service launched; West Coast expresses run at 110mph.

May 14 Last vacuum-braked wagonload train.

July 4 New BREL International coach with export order potential.

July 6 RETB signalling pioneered between Inverness–Kyle of Lochalsh.

July 13 Polmont (Scotland) crash; thirteen die when push-pull train hits cow.

July 17 Mock high-speed crash to demonstrate strength and safety of nuclear flasks.

July 27 East Coast electrification approved. Cost: £306million.

August 30 Western HST sets world diesel speed record, Paddington–Bristol (average of 112.8mph).

November 19 £360million total DMU replacement policy announced.

December 7 BR's last 1,500V DC trains run between Manchester Piccadilly–Hadfield.

December 12 Euston–Glasgow record run of 3hr 52.75min by APT.

1985

January 3 ScotRail brand name launched.

January 20 Enthusiasts mourn last BR passenger runs of Class 40 diesels.

March 18 Dornoch bridge diversion proposed for Far North line. Money not ultimately raised and new bridge built for road only.

March 23 Last runs of LMS-design EMUs on Merseyside.

May 7 Work starts on East Coast electrification at Hitchin.

May 13 Mark 3 Pullman services introduced.

May 15 Closure announced of BREL Swindon Works.

May 17 Dundee power box opened.

July 15 First modular catering on InterCity services.

July 20 Waterloo–Bournemouth speed record of 83min 25.2sec.

1986

January 12 Cross-London BR travellers offered free travel on the Underground.

January 20 Anglo-French Channel Tunnel agreement signed.

January 21 American-built Class 59 locomotives arrive for Foster Yeoman.

March 16 Energisation of Tonbridge–Hastings line, followed by Wickford–Southminster (March 17), Manningtree–Harwich (March 24).

April 1 BREL restructured into two groups as prelude to privatisation.

June 10 Launch of Network SouthEast.

June 24 APT vehicles sold for scrap.

September 19 High-speed collision at Colwich, Staffs.

September 28 Launch of Ayrshire electric service.

November 19 Leicester resignalling switched in.

1987

February 7 New Bishop's Stortford–Stansted Airport rail link authorised.

April 1 BR introduces new depot/works maintenance policy.

May 1 InterCity 21st anniversary celebrations.

May 11 End of East Coast main line sleeper services, diverted to Euston.

May 5 First London–Norwich electric breaks time record with 83min 22sec.

July 3 Outline approval for Manchester LRT system.

October 2 Rebuilt Snow Hill, Birmingham, opened on site of GWR station closed 1972.

October 11 Marylebone and Chiltern lines transferred to Western Region.

October 16 100mph storms bring chaos to South East.

October 19 Glanrhyd bridge collapse on Central Wales line. Four killed.

November 18 King's Cross Underground fire. Though not BR, it had significant effect on all underground working practices, eg roof work on underground sections at Birmingham New Street and spread of non-smoking restrictions.

December 6 Leicester resignalling scheme complete.

1988

January 11 Bournemouth–Weymouth electrification completed.

February 22 First through West Coast–East Anglia electrically hauled freights via North London line.

February 29 213th and final BR steam loco sold from Barry scrapyard.

March 13 Death of former BR chairman Sir Henry Johnson.

April 1 New Anglia Region breaks away from the Eastern.

May 20 BR chairman Sir Robert Reid opens historic Malvern station rebuilt after fire.

May 28 RETB signalling introduced to West Highland Line.

June 2 Go-ahead for £2 billion redevelopment of King's Cross site.

June 6 BR invites tenders for sale of its last remaining steam line, the Vale of Rheidol.

July 3 First electric service to Doncaster on 50th anniversary of world speed record run by LNER Class A4 4-6-2 No 4468 *Mallard* (also in attendance).

August 5 Settle & Carlisle Line offered for sale.

August 11 First electric train to Leeds.

October 16 LNER Class A3 4-6-2 No 4472 *Flying Scotsman* starts year tour of Australia.

November 5 Last timetabled BR steam trains on Vale of Rheidol line prior to sale.

December 13 Clapham Junction disaster. Thirt-five killed.

1989

January 26 'Battersea Bullet' private leisure trains ordered from BREL.

February 7 Collapse of Ness Viaduct, Inverness, isolates Far North lines. But new summer service with Sprinters goes ahead while bridge rebuilt.

March 4 Purley accident. Six killed, 80 injured.

March 8 Proposed Channel Tunnel high-speed route angers Kent residents.

April 11 Settle & Carlisle Line reprieved as part of BR.

September 17 Class 91 loco achieves 162mph on test near Grantham.

October 2 Leeds electric service inaugurated with new Mark 4 coaches. First electric trains reach York.

October 12 Conservative Government postpones BR privatisation proposals.

November 9 Breakthrough of first Channel Tunnel service tunnel between Folkestone and dover.

December New chairman of Rail Board announced, Robert Reid (of Shell) to replace Sir Bob Reid (no relationship) October 1990.

ACKNOWLEDGEMENTS

Photographs are by: H. Ballantyne (2 both, 6 lower, 7 both, 8 upper, 11 lower, 12, 14 upper, 15 lower, 18 upper, 21 both, 42, 46, 52, 59 lower, 61, 62, 71, 79, 83, 93, 95, 97 upper, 112, 118, 120, 132, 135 upper, 136, 139 upper, 145, 148, 150, 151 both, 152, 154 both, 161, 173, 177 both); British Rail (76, 165); British Rail/G. M. Kichenside (125 both, 128); British Rail/ Neil Wooler (103, 104, 106, 109 both); Eurotunnel (184); Festiniog Railway (176); P. J. Howard (31 upper); J. Makepeace (11 upper); I. McDonald (15 upper); B. Morrison (28, 55, 60, 80, 84, 87, 88, 90, 94, 131, 139 lower, 141, 142, 146, 147, 156, 158 both); R. W. Penny (174 both); P. J. Robinson (8 lower, 13, 17, 18 lower, 19 both, 22 both, 23 both, 24, 26 both, 27 both, 30 both, 31 lower, 32, 35, 36, 38, 39, 40, 43, 45, 49, 50, 51, 56, 59 upper, 67, 68, 72, 75, 97 lower, 98, 100, 101, 123, 129, 135 lower); K. Sanders (14 lower); P. Shannon (111, 115, 117 both, 119, 121); J. Smart (6 upper); Times Newspapers (168); E. Treacy (178).

INDEX

Page references in *italic* denote illustrations